$4 —
HAB

11/22

A PEOPLE
ON THE MOVE
The Métis of the Western Plains

IRENE TERNIER GORDON

VICTORIA · VANCOUVER · CALGARY

Heritage House Publishing Company Ltd.
#108 – 17665 66A Avenue
Surrey, BC V3S 2A7
www.heritagehouse.ca

Heritage House Publishing Company Ltd.
PO Box 468
Custer, WA
98240-0468

Library and Archives Canada Cataloguing in Publication
Gordon, Irene Ternier
    A people on the move: the Métis of the western plains / Irene Gordon.

Includes bibliographical references.
ISBN 978-1-894974-85-1

    1. Métis—Prairie Provinces—History—19th century. 2. Métis—Prairie Provinces—Biography.
3. Prairie Provinces—History—19th century.

FC109.G64 2009   971.2004'97   C2008-908119-6

Library of Congress Control Number: 2009920302

Series editor: Lesley Reynolds.
Cover design: Chyla Cardinal. Interior design: Frances Hunter.
Cover photo: Gabriel Dumont, Glenbow Archives (NA-1063-1). Interior photos: Provincial Archives of Manitoba, page 11 (SIS 911932), page 40 (SIS N4035), page 76 (SIS N14689); Glenbow Archives, page 25 (NA-1185-5), page 59 (NA-1337-3); Saskatchewan Archives Board, page 93 (R-A6277), page 127 (R-A3465). Map: Real Bérard. © Guillaume Charette, 1976. First published in *Vanishing Spaces: Memoirs of Louis Goulet, a Prairie Métis*, Editions Bois-Brûlés. This work is protected by copyright and the making of this copy was with the permission of Access Copyright. Any alteration of its content or further copying in any form whatsoever is strictly prohibited unless otherwise permitted by law.

Mixed Sources
Cert no. SW-COC-001271
© 1996 FSC
FSC

The interior of this book was printed on 100% post-consumer recycled paper, processed chlorine free and printed with vegetable-based inks.

Heritage House acknowledges the financial support for its publishing program from the Government of Canada through the Book Publishing Industry Development Program (BPIDP), Canada Council for the Arts and the province of British Columbia through the British Columbia Arts Council and the Book Publishing Tax Credit.

BRITISH COLUMBIA
ARTS COUNCIL

The Canada Council | Le Conseil des Arts
for the Arts | du Canada

12 11 10 09   1 2 3 4 5
Printed in Canada

Contents

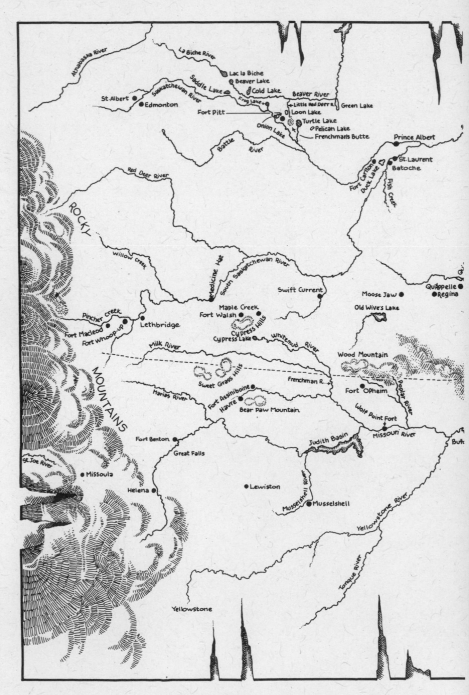

The Prairies from the Red River to the Rocky Mountains *circa* 1850–1900.
The western three-quarters of this area is known as the western plains.

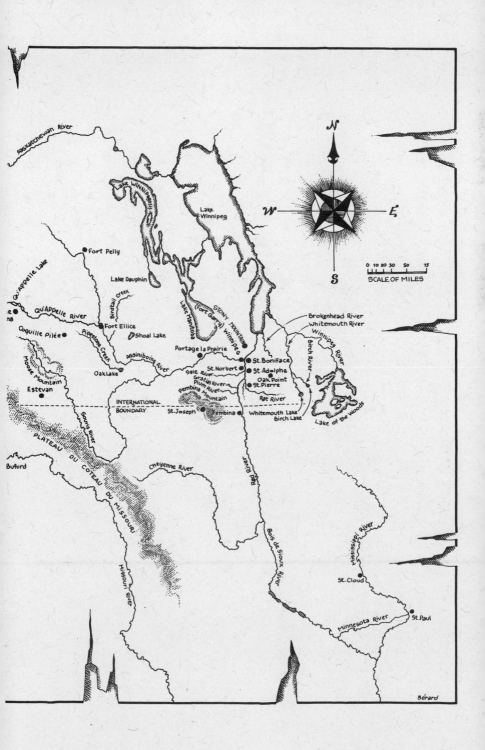

*To the descendants of the Métis of the western plains
who people this book—most especially to members of the Boyer,
Nolin, Delorme, Ness and Pruden families with whom
I attended school and church while I was growing up at
Cochin, Saskatchewan.*

Prologue

IT WAS LATE AFTERNOON ON *Saturday, July 12, 1851. Scouts from the St. François Xavier buffalo-hunting party had just reached the top of the first terrace of the Grand Coteau of the Missouri River. They caught sight of a large Sioux encampment and signalled back to the rest of the group. Jean-Baptiste Falcon, chief of the hunt, ordered camp be made immediately and that it be put in defensive mode.*

Falcon sent five scouts with a spyglass to check out the Sioux camp. They rode to the top of the nearest high bluff and looked down on a camp that they estimated to hold at least 2,000 warriors. The scouts, scorning concealment, rode boldly toward the camp. A party of 20 Sioux rode out to meet them. When the two groups met, the Sioux surrounded the Métis and invited them to accompany them to their camp.

Two of the Métis, realizing that the Sioux considered them prisoners, suddenly kicked their horses into a gallop and escaped under fire back to their camp. The Sioux followed. They assured Falcon that they had peaceful intentions, but said that they were hard up and needed help. They promised that a small party of them would return the next day to release the three remaining prisoners in exchange for gifts.

The Métis did not believe the Sioux promise, but they did not expect trouble until the next day because the Sioux did not fight at night. After dark, two men were sent to the main party of buffalo hunters, some 12 to 18 kilometres away, to ask for help. Could they arrive back with reinforcements in time?

Early Sunday morning, Father LaFlèche, who was travelling with the hunters, said Mass. Shortly afterwards, the Sioux arrived—not the promised small group, but a whole army of men shouting and brandishing weapons that glinted in the fierce morning sunlight.

Falcon sent 30 of the hunters out to meet the Sioux.

CHAPTER

1

Who Are the Métis?

"They one and all look upon themselves as members of an independent tribe of natives entitled to a property in the soil, a flag of their own, and to protection from the British government."

—WILLIAM MCGILLIVRAY,
NOR'WEST COMPANY HEAD, 1818

WHO ARE THE MÉTIS? THE simple answer is that they are the offspring of First Nations women and European men, the first of whom were born precisely nine months after the first Europeans set foot in North America. Not counting the visits of the Vikings *circa* 1000, this was around 1500 in eastern North America and 1670 in the West. Racial mixing alone does not produce a new people, however. At first, mixed-race children normally assimilated into the society of one of the parents. While a small number of boys went to Europe or the Canadas for an education, and some girls married their father's fur-trade colleagues, most early western Métis lived the lifestyle of their Native mothers. However, by 1812, when Lord Selkirk established the Red River Settlement at the site of present-day Winnipeg, the Métis were well recognized as a culturally distinct people.

According to most historians, this happened only in the Canadian West (and a narrow strip south of the Canadian-American border), where the Métis carved out a distinctive economic niche for themselves in the fur trade by manning the brigades hauling supplies and furs, hunting buffalo and making pemmican. The Métis even had their own language, called Michif, which uses French nouns and Cree verbs plus some words from other Native languages.

Métis society became different from either parent society largely due to the nature of the founding fathers of the Métis nation. These men left their homes in Quebec or the British Isles to explore and participate in the fur trade. As such, they were often the bravest and most independent and adventuresome of their communities.

The North West (or Nor'West) Company strongly opposed the establishment of the Red River Settlement because it believed that agriculture would damage the fur trade. It encouraged the Métis to join in a campaign against the settlement. Nor'West leaders named four captains to lead the Métis: Cuthbert Grant Jr., William Shaw, Pierre "Bostonnais" Pangman and Nicholas "Bonhomme"

This photograph of Métis traders at their campsite was taken by the Boundary Commission photographer between 1872 and 1874, possibly in the Wood Mountain area.

Montour. These men, all sons of Nor'West employees, described themselves as "the four chiefs of the half-Indians by the mutual consent of their fellows." In addition to demanding that the settlers be removed, the chiefs also insisted that the Métis keep "the full liberty of running buffalo and living according to the custom in which they have been brought up."

Louis Riel is the first person known to have used

"Métis" (an old French word meaning "of mixed race"), in an article published not long after his death in November 1885. There is no single agreed-upon definition of Métis today. A minority would argue that the only true Métis are directly descended from a French-Canadian father and a Cree or Ojibwa mother, but most people accept a broader definition. The Métis Nation-Saskatchewan Constitution defines a Métis as: an Aboriginal person who "self-identifies as Métis" and is either a descendant of those Métis who "were entitled to receive land grants and/or Scrip under the provision of the Manitoba Act, 1870 or the Dominion Lands Act "; or "a person of Aboriginal descent who is accepted by the Métis Nation and/or Métis Community."

A missionary named Father Belcourt wrote in the 1850s that the Métis were "endowed with uncommon health and strength [and] esteem themselves the lords of the land . . . Their character is gentle and benevolent . . . they are capable of enduring . . . the most horrible fatigues and they undertake them with the greatest cheerfulness when circumstances call for it."

In the following pages are the stories of the Métis of the western plains (what became the provinces of Saskatchewan and Alberta in 1905). Many of them migrated from the Red River or were descendants of the Red River Métis. The blossoming of their society and culture marked a fascinating and colourful era in Canadian history.

2

Eat, Drink and Be Merry

*"One of my interpreters has taken one of the native's daughters
for a wife . . . all the ceremonies attending to [a marriage]
are that when it becomes time to retire, the husband . . . shews
his bride where his bed is, and then they . . . go to rest together,
and they continue to do so long as they can agree among
themselves, but when either is displeased with their choice he
or she will seek another partner."*

—DANIEL HARMON,
NOR'WEST COMPANY FUR TRADER

SHORTLY AFTER HARMON WROTE THE above journal entry
describing an 1801 wedding, a Cree chief offered his daughter to Harmon as a wife. "He pressed me to keep her . . . he
said he was fond of me, and he wished to have his daughter
with the white people." Harmon almost accepted the offer
because he was lonely and the marriage would have been
good for his business. "While I had the daughter I should

not only have the father's hunts, but those of his relations also." Harmon, however, was a very religious man who did not believe it would be right to take a wife without marrying her in a religious ceremony.

In 1805, Harmon finally broke down and accepted a 14-year-old girl named Lisette (Lizette) Duval as a wife. She was the daughter of a French-Canadian father and a Snake mother. "The girl is said to be of a mild disposition and even tempered, which are qualities very necessary to make an agreeable woman and an affectionate partner," he wrote of her. Originally, Harmon had planned to place Lisette "into the hands of some good honest man, with whom she can pass the remainder of her days" when he left the fur trade. When that time came, however, he had changed his mind and asked her to marry him in a religious ceremony. He could not imagine breaking up their family because he and Lisette had "wept together over the earthly departure of several children" and their living children were "equally dear" to both of them.

The Harmons were formally married at Fort William in 1819. They had six more children before moving to a farm near Montreal in 1843. Harmon and several of the children died a few weeks later of either smallpox or scarlet fever. Lisette, who lived for another 19 years, remained in the Montreal area. She outlived all but one of her 14 children.

Marriage à la façon du pays

Marriages like those of Harmon and his interpreter were known as country marriages (*marriage à la façon du pays*). Initially, First Nations people encouraged such unions for their daughters. Marriage to a fur trader worked to the economic benefit of both sides. The First Nations people expected to have free access to the fur-trade post and provisions, while the trader expected the marriage to strengthen trading ties with his wife's extended family or tribe. The trader also gained a helpmate skilled in the many tasks essential for daily life in fur-trade country, a companion and sexual partner, and a mother for his children.

If a trader wanted a First Nations wife, he first had to gain her parents' consent and pay a bride price determined by her relatives, which often was a horse. The men then smoked a calumet (pipe) together to seal the agreement. When the trader came to claim his bride, the couple would be ceremoniously escorted to the fort. The new bride was usually taken through a cleansing rite by the other women of the fort and given new clothing of a more European style.

Girls were married at a very young age. A visitor to Cumberland House in 1819 said that girls "are frequently wives at 12 years of age and mothers at 14." He said that instances were known where the master of a post had permitted a voyageur "to take to wife a poor child that had scarcely attained the age of 10 years." It is possible, however, that in some of these cases the man may have acted as a guardian to a young girl until she was considered mature enough to marry.

That may have been the situation with Nor'West trader John MacDonnell and his wife, Magdeleine Poitras, who had their first child when Magdeleine was 16. MacDonnell wrote to his brother in June 1812 that he was moving his wife and children to the Ottawa River on his retirement. He added that "the mother has been my constant companion these 18 years and under my protection since her 12th year."

Country marriages may have been happy and successful, or may have ended in cruelty or desertion, but little is known about most of them. Although many fur traders kept detailed journals, they rarely mentioned their wives. Harmon only mentioned his wife four times and never called her by name. He did say, however, that it was a mark of respect among the Cree not to speak the name of a person under discussion.

Even less is known about the women's feelings. One exception is Harriet Vincent. Many years later, she confided the details of her unhappy first marriage, telling how she was dragged forcibly from her mother when her father gave her in marriage at the age of 12. She declared that she never hated any other man as she did her first husband, who "beat and maltreated her till life was a burden." After nine miserable years, she was abandoned. Four years later, she married a chief trader named George Gladman Jr. That was a much happier marriage. Harriet said of her two husbands that she "was sent" with the first, but that she "went" with the second.

Harriet also said that her parents' marriage ended unhappily after many years when her father took a second wife. According to Harriet, her country-born (mixed-blood) mother, Jane Renton, took in a young widow to help with the work, and said widow "prevailed upon her father to take her too." As a result, Jane "got indignant" and left her English-born husband, Thomas Vincent.

Peter Fidler was an English-born trader and surveyor who worked for the Hudson's Bay Company (HBC). He and his Cree wife, Mary, who were married in a religious ceremony in 1821, seem to have had a successful marriage. Fidler recalled that when they were originally married at York Factory in 1794, he had given a gun to Mary's father and a knife and some awls to her mother. Then they had rejoiced around a keg of rum with her family. While Fidler rarely mentioned his wife in his journal, he kept a detailed record of the births of his 14 children. The record began with Thomas, born at York Factory on June 20, 1795, at eight minutes past midnight. It ended with Harriet, born at Dauphin House on July 9, 1822, at 4:53.

As time went on, traders became more likely to marry Métis rather than First Nations women, and marriage rites took on a more European form with vows taken before witnesses. After 1821, the HBC introduced a marriage contract. Some HBC factors (the men in charge of the trading posts) were named Justices of the Peace and were thus empowered to perform marriages.

A contract from Oxford House in 1830 stated: "This is to certify that I, Magnus Harper . . . have taken to wife, for better or worse Peggy La Pierre . . . and I, by this document do hereby bind and promise to cherish and support the said Peggy La Pierre as my lawful married wife during the term of her natural life." With the arrival of missionaries, a clause was sometimes added stating that the couple would be married by a clergyman as soon as possible.

Although Chief Factor John Rowand did not choose to have a religious marriage ceremony when a missionary visited Fort Edmonton, he remained loyal to his wife, Louise, until her death. In writing of her death in 1849, he deplored the loss of "my old friend and mother of all my children." In his will he described his children as "reputed," a term often used to indicate that a church marriage had not occurred. John Edward Harriott, who married Rowand's daughter Nancy, said that he would submit to a church wedding only "to please people and to conform to the custom of society [but] I would not consider myself more strongly bound to the woman than before."

HBC governor George Simpson, who had abandoned several country wives and imported an English bride, later became more favourably disposed to Métis wives—at least for other men. He complained in 1848 about an employee who brought his British wife to live at Moose Factory. When men "choose to marry in the country, there can be no great objection to it because native women are tolerably manageable; but imported wives fancy themselves such great women that there is no possibility of pleasing them."

Courtship Métis Style

Winter was the prime time for Métis courtship and marriage, as during the rest of the year many people were away from home on the buffalo hunt or freighting. George William Sanderson, who was courting his wife in the 1860s, said that lack of privacy and a shortage of girls made courting difficult for him. "The old ladies were very stingy of their daughters, and a fellow had a hard time to get a chance to talk to one alone," he complained. He would have liked to take his girl out for a drive, but a Red River cart was his only conveyance, "and they squealed so you couldn't hear anything." Despite these handicaps, George was married in 1867.

Courtship was carried on in public because houses were small and families large. A visitor to the North-West, Henry Martin Robinson, described the courtship of a couple (whom he called Gabriel and Philomel) that he observed while a guest in the girl's home. Gabriel arrived at Philomel's home in the early evening. On his arrival, every member of the family, including her two younger brothers and her seven sisters, either shook Gabriel's hand or hugged him. Then Philomel's mother invited him to sit down and eat, despite the fact that both he and Philomel's family had barely finished supper. Gabriel naturally accepted, and Philomel's father ate with him while the women of the family waited upon them.

Once the two men finished their second supper, his prospective father-in-law invited Gabriel to have a smoke. Philomel quickly cleared the table and retired to the most secluded corner of the room, where Gabriel later joined her. The remainder of the family suddenly acted as though the young couple were invisible. The father and Robinson enjoyed a drink of rum, the brothers played noisily together, the sisters quietly commented among themselves on Gabriel's looks and wardrobe, and the mother busied herself with some mending.

At first, Gabriel found it difficult to ignore the presence of Philomel's family and contented himself with looking admiringly at her. As the evening wore on, however, he gained courage and declared his love for her. Immediately, all of Philomel's female relatives gathered around the young couple to console themselves on the prospect of losing her and to congratulate Gabriel on gaining her affections.

After a few more such evening visits, Philomel's mother proudly showed Gabriel the household goods that Philomel would take to her new home once she was married. They included a feather bed, earthenware dishes and tin cooking pots. Then Philomel's father presented Gabriel with a gun and drank to his health before the family sat down to supper. The young couple were now officially engaged. For his part, Gabriel prepared for his wedding by laying in a supply of buffalo meat and rum for the wedding feast, to which everyone in the community was invited. On his wedding day, he would have presented his new father-in-law with a few ponies or some provisions.

A Métis Ball

Robinson eagerly accepted an invitation to attend a party in celebration of the engagement of another young woman he called Pauline Pirouette. Each arriving male guest was greeted with "sweet smiles" by the women and boisterous horseplay by the other men before being conducted into the house and offered a drink.

Pauline greeted Robinson "with charming familiarity" while "talking earnestly and incoherently" about her sweetheart. Then she conducted him to the kitchen, where he paid his respects to her mother. Delicious odours rose from the kettles and the numerous spits turning slowly before the huge fireplace. Mme. Pirouette greeted Robinson cordially with a hug and kisses on both cheeks. To his alarm, she came close to putting his eyes out with the knife and fork she was holding.

Just then, the tuning of a fiddle indicated that the dance was about to begin. A pair of dancers got up on the floor and "after a preliminary courtesy" began to do the Red River jig while the remaining guests looked on admiringly. After a few minutes, an onlooker replaced the first male dancer. Shortly afterwards, another girl replaced the first girl. This continued until everyone had their turn. Certain performers tested their legs and wind "by earnest efforts to dance each other down," and the audience encouraged their favourites. One popular female dancer received such comments as, "Oh, my little dear! What legs you have got! You are entirely too much for that little frog! When you are done, you shall have a drink, my daughter."

Following the jig came reels performed by six or eight dancers, who gave way to other dancers when they became exhausted. Robinson invited Pauline to dance the reel, but he found himself no match for her. Soon she swung him off the floor and made to sit on his knee. "That being a weak point in my anatomy, I forego the pleasure by sliding quickly to the end of the box," he observed ruefully.

After a supper of various meats and bannock, the dance continued with "unabated vigour." Robinson noticed, however, the mysterious disappearance and reappearance of dancers. Curious, he followed one disappearing dancer to a distant part of the house and found the missing guests stretched out on the floor asleep—males in one room and females in another.

When Robinson woke in the morning, he was surprised to find that the young people who danced through the night had been replaced by a set of older people. They danced throughout the day, and at night the young people began again. After three days, everyone finally headed home.

A member of a visiting scientific expedition described two dances he had attended in the 1850s. When he arrived at the first dance, attended by the "commonalty," some 20 or 30 people were sitting around the room on the floor. The dance began with jigs, reels and quadrilles danced in rapid succession. The writer described the scene somewhat fancifully:

> A black-eyed beauty in blue calico and a strapping Bois-Brûlé would jump up from the floor and outdo their predecessors in figure and velocity, the lights and shadows chasing each other faster and faster over the rafters; the flame, too, swaying wildly hither and thither; and above the thumps of the dancers' heels and the frequent 'Ho! Ho!' rose the monomaniac fiddle-shrieks of the trembling strings, as if the devil was at the bow.

The following night a second dance took place for the "aristocracy" of the community. Here the writer found "a better fiddle, and a better fiddler, and better dancing." The best dancers were an 11-year-old boy and his grandfather—the son and father-in-law of the host. "The latter was as tireless as if his aged limbs had lost no strength, and little Joe had extra double-shuffles and intricate steps, and miraculously lively movements."

Christmas and New Year's Celebrations

The Métis love of food and dance was particularly evident at Christmas and the New Year. The artist Paul Kane, who spent December 1847 at Fort Edmonton, was invited to have Christmas dinner with Chief Factor John Edward Harriott. Harriott's Métis wife, Nancy, daughter of John Rowand, was apparently not at the dinner, as men and women rarely ate together at the factor's table. The menu included boiled buffalo hump, boiled buffalo calf (taken by Caesarean section from the mother long before reaching full size), *mouffle* (dried moose nose), buffalo tongue, beaver tails, roast wild goose, potatoes, turnips, bread and whitefish fried in buffalo marrow. There were no desserts.

The day ended with a dance attended by everyone in the fort. All the guests were dressed in their brightest finery—the Native people with faces painted, Canadian voyageurs "with bright sashes and neatly ornamented moccasins" and the Métis "glittering in every ornament they could lay their hands on." Kane occasionally led a young woman out onto the dance floor, although none of the women spoke English. They danced to "highland-reel" tunes which the fiddler played with great vigour. The women, with grave faces, "kept jumping up and down, both feet off the ground at once" while Kane danced around them "with all the agility" he was capable of. Kane was so taken with the beauty of a young Métis woman named Cun-ne-wa-bum (One Who Looks at the Stars) that he later painted a picture of her

Métis New Year's Day celebrations at Lac La Biche, 1895, drawn by Frederick Remington.

holding a fan made from the tip of a swan's wing with a porcupine-quill handle.

Country-born interpreter Peter Erasmus and his employer, a Methodist missionary named Reverend Thomas Woolsey, spent Christmas 1856 at Fort Edmonton. Erasmus recalled the growing excitement and hustle among the fort residents, as HBC officials from all the surrounding posts customarily met at Fort Edmonton over Christmas week for combined business meetings and celebrations. The dog drivers were rushing supplies of fish to the fort to feed the visitors' dogs. Erasmus and two other men went to hunt for buffalo, returning four days later with two fine cows. He reported, "Every arrival was a signal for all the dogs of the fort and those of the Crees camped nearby to raise their voices in a deafening uproar of welcome or defiance as their tempers dictated."

Erasmus "was burning to go" to the Christmas dance, but he knew that Woolsey strongly objected to dancing. Finally, Erasmus "screwed up his courage" and asked for permission to attend. Woolsey grudgingly agreed as long as Erasmus promised not to drink any alcohol. This he agreed to readily, as he did not drink.

Shortly after breakfast on Christmas Eve, a horn signalled that the factor was ready to receive "the salutations of the men at the fort." The chief clerk greeted each man in turn and handed him a ration of rum, which company rules stated was not to be touched until Christmas Day. Erasmus shook hands with the factor, but refused the customary drink. Bill Borwick, Erasmus' roommate during his stay at the fort, was furious. He told Erasmus that he was guilty of a grave discourtesy toward the company officials. Erasmus retorted that he did not work for the HBC and that his first duty was to his employer.

On Christmas morning, Erasmus was awakened from a deep sleep by "a tremendous bloodcurdling noise." By the time he had scrambled into his clothes and gone outside, he realized he was hearing, for the first time, the sound of bagpipes echoing back from the "high hills of the ice-covered

Saskatchewan." They were played by a kilted piper, seemingly oblivious to the -35°C cold on his bare knees. Erasmus quickly reversed his first opinion of the bagpipes, saying the sound "was beautiful, even to my unfamiliar ears."

Christmas Day was spent visiting, followed by a dance in the evening. At midnight a big potluck lunch was served in the homes of the married couples. The single men were kept so busy acting as errand boys that they were unable to share in the talk or food. Erasmus was getting a bit annoyed, but Borwick told him to be patient. Finally, the dancing began again. Then Erasmus and Borwick found themselves the only men at a table being plied with food and conversation by three very attractive waitresses. The dance did not end until daylight.

The chief factor at Fort Carlton described the New Year's celebrations there in 1825. The day began with the men firing a salute of musketry "at our doors and windows." Then they came into the hall "to wish us the compliments of the season." There, the men were "liberally treated" with shrub (a cordial of fruit juice and alcohol), rum and cakes. They fired a second salute as they left. Then the women arrived. Each was kissed *à la mode du pays* (on both cheeks) and treated with cakes and shrub. At 4 p.m. the men assembled for a feast, complete with plum pudding. Afterwards, they sang songs in Gaelic and French while their wives had dinner. Finally, the men and women joined together for a dance.

Food and Drink

Contemporary accounts of their feasts and celebrations show that the Métis were renowned for their hearty appetites. Robinson noted, "If a Métis can starve better than any other man, he can equally surpass other men in the quantity of food he can consume at a sitting."

A recent convert once told a missionary priest that he did not require so much food since he had become a Christian. The man said that when he followed the religion of his mother, he could eat eight rabbits for his dinner and still was not satisfied. "But since I have become a Christian . . . six rabbits at a time is plenty for me; I don't want any more!" he concluded proudly.

Frequently, the guests at a party consumed the host family's provisions for the entire winter. For the remainder of the winter, this family would be entertained in turn by their neighbours in equally lavish style.

The Métis often relied on pemmican for sustenance. A mixture of dried buffalo meat mixed with fat and wild berries, pemmican was the fuel that ran the fur trade. It was an almost ideal food—cheap, easily transported and it did not spoil if made and stored properly. One kilogram of pemmican was nutritionally equivalent to at least three or four times that weight of fresh meat.

Once buffalo carcasses were safely in camp after a day's hunt, the women prepared the meat. The tongue and the hump, considered delicacies, were usually eaten fresh, or the tongue was pickled in brine. All other meat not eaten immediately was cut into long, narrow strips and hung on wooden racks to dry in the sun. After a few days, the strips were broken into equal lengths and tied into 25- or 30-kilogram bundles called *viande seche* (dried meat) for transportation home. Meat to be made into pemmican immediately was further dried over a slow fire until it became brittle enough to be pounded into flakes or powder. Melted tallow or bone-marrow fat and berries were mixed into the meat, and the warm pemmican was packed into parfleches (untanned buffalo skin bags), about the size of pillow cases. The parfleches were sealed with melted tallow, sewn shut and compacted to about a 15- to 18-centimetre thickness. Each sack weighed about 45 kilograms.

Pemmican made within a fort was generally superior to that made in the camp, where the meat may have been pounded on a none-too-clean buffalo hide, and the wind might have mixed dirt and other debris with the meat. Some people said that well-made pemmican was delicious. Others agreed with the man who said, "Take the scrapings from . . . a very stale piece of cold roast beef, add to it lumps of . . . rancid fat . . . then garnish with human . . . dog and oxen hairs and you have pemmican."

Although pemmican was often eaten out of hand by travellers, it was usually fried or cooked into a stew called *rubaboo*. To make *rubaboo*, a lump of pemmican was chopped up and boiled with flour and whatever vegetables and seasonings were available. Fried pemmican, or *rechaud*, also often had flour and seasoning added. Bread made with yeast was unknown. Bannock—a biscuit made of flour, fat, water and leavening that could be fried, baked or cooked on a stick over a campfire—was eaten instead.

Norbert Welsh described some of the traditional foods his wife, Cecilia, made for special occasions. For the main course she would serve *des boulettes* (meatballs) of chopped buffalo meat boiled with potatoes. For dessert she made *la poutine dans le sac* (suet pudding) with raisins and brandy sauce. *De croxegnols*, a New Year's treat similar to dough-nuts, were a particular favourite of the Welsh children. The children sometimes even climbed onto the roof of the house and ran sharp sticks down the chimney in an attempt to spear the *croxegnols* out of the pot of boiling oil as their mother cooked them.

Tea was considered an essential part of every meal. Well-known missionary priest Father Albert Lacombe quipped that tea drinking was the only form of atheism practiced by the Métis. He called them *"un peuple à thé"* (a tea-loving people), as opposed to *"un peuple athée"* (an atheistic people).

Victoria Callihoo (née Belcourt) described the traditional diet from her childhood in central Alberta in the 1860s and 1870s. The only items her parents traded for at the local HBC store were "fancy extras" such as tea and sugar. For meat, they hunted big game, ducks and geese. They grew potatoes, cabbages, carrots and onions in their garden. They also grew barley, which they boiled in soup or roasted and drank like coffee, and dried wild berries for winter use or to add to pemmican. Women who were lucky enough to have glass jars made preserves. One kind of preserve, called "scratch," was made out of chokecherries. It included the stones, which were "bashed into tiny pieces" for extra flavour. Birch and poplar sap were used for sweetening instead of sugar.

Clothing, the Sash and "The Flower Beadwork People"

When Métis people gathered to eat, drink and dance, they dressed for the occasion. Some Métis wore traditional First Nations clothing, others adopted European styles, while a third group combined European and Native dress to create a distinctively colourful and flamboyant Métis style. Gabriel and Philomel's wedding finery was in typical Métis style. Gabriel was particularly proud of his new *mitasses* (leggings) and Red River coat made for the occasion by his mother.

For her wedding, Philomel wore a dark dress brightened by a coloured head scarf and beautifully embroidered moccasins. Robinson commented that after her wedding Philomel "will remove the gaudy handkerchief from her head, and wear it crossed meekly upon her breast in token of her wifehood."

Women tended to wear less brightly coloured and ornamented clothing than men. Black velvet was a favourite material. Their relatively austere clothing may have been

due to the influence of the Grey Nuns, who provided whatever education young girls received. They wore gathered
skirts and full-sleeved blouses known as basques. Like the
men, they usually wore beaded moccasins and leggings.
Métis women covered their heads with shawls or scarves
and often wore a blanket or shawl instead of a coat.

There were three styles of men's coats. The leather Red
River coat, which had shoulder epaulets and a fitted waist,
flared out over the hips and was lavishly decorated with
stylized beadwork flowers. The buckskin jacket, decorated
with fringes and beadwork, was widely manufactured and
sold by Métis women. Pictures of men like Gabriel Dumont
and Buffalo Bill often show them wearing such jackets.
The capote, a long, hooded jacket made from a Hudson's
Bay blanket and fastened with a sash, was the final type.
Mitasses, the most prized possession of many men, were
usually saved to be worn to special social events and to
church. They fit snugly from ankle to knee and were made
of leather or, more commonly, of black velvet and decorated
with beadwork and embroidery. By the 1870s, hide clothing
had almost been completely replaced by fabric, and women
preferred European-style clothing.

The Métis were extremely fond of beadwork. Clothing,
saddles and bags for carrying gunpowder and tobacco were
all decorated with brightly coloured beadwork, often with a
floral motif. As a result, the Sioux gave the Métis the nick-
name "The Flower Beadwork People." It is possible that this

style of beadwork originated in Quebec and was taught by the Grey Nuns to their female students.

Perhaps the most recognizable Métis symbol today is the sash. The ceinture fléchée (arrow belt) was brought west by their French-Canadian forefathers. It was also known as the L'Assomption Sash after the Quebec town where it was produced. First Nations and Métis women began to finger-weave these sashes after they gained access to wool through the fur trade, and individual families soon developed their own distinctive design and colour combinations. Sashes were commonly about 15 centimetres wide and from 2 to 6 metres in length. A typical sash had a red band in the centre with zigzags forming an arrow design on both sides. The best quality sashes were so tightly woven of waxed wool that they could hold water. Originally, sashes were much more than a decorative belt. They could be used instead of rope, as a tumpline when carrying heavy loads over portages, like a pocket to carry small items, as a dog harness or instead of a towel. The fringes could be used as thread for emergency repairs.

Housing

While Métis feasts and clothing were often elaborate, the same could not usually be said of their homes. Generally, the Métis lived in small houses furnished with simple home-made furniture. This was particularly true of those who followed the buffalo hunt and camped in tents for much of the summer. Many of the hunters, who became known as *hiverants* (winterers), preferred to stay out on the prairie over the winter rather than return to their permanent homes. They built small communities of long, narrow huts with flat, sod-covered roofs. A visiting priest described these cabins as looking like giant coffins. Most held one or two families, but sometimes multi-family cabins were built. The *hiverant* community of Chapel Coulee, which was home to some 60 families in the 1870s, only had 15 houses. Each house was approximately 4 by 12 metres and partitioned into four separate apartments. Most communities also included two larger buildings: one that served as a church and home for the travelling missionary priest, and one that was a store and home for a free trader. Over the years, some of these winter communities evolved into permanent settlements, while others disappeared.

Henry Martin Robinson spent the night in one of these winter homes when he was caught in a blizzard. The interior walls of the one-room cabin were plastered with mud and buffalo hair, and a buffalo robe served for a door. The pounded earth floor was dug down below ground level to keep out drafts and give more headroom. The only furnishings were a narrow bedstead painted a vivid blue, a table and two chairs, a few wooden boxes and an open fireplace. Several brightly coloured religious pictures and a rosary decorated the wall over the bed.

After a meagre supper of fish without salt, Robinson began to wonder if they would have to sit up all night since there was only one bed to accommodate 15 people—the host couple, their 11 children, Robinson and his guide. Just then, the lady of the house asked the children sitting on the boxes to stand up. Then she and the older daughters pulled blankets and fur robes from the boxes. In a few minutes, the robes were spread out on the floor and Robinson found himself "the central figure in a closely-packed bed of 13." Except for the parents, who occupied the bright blue bed, everyone slept on the floor.

Victoria Callihoo described the home of her early childhood in Alberta as a log house with buffalo parchment windows (a buffalo hide scraped very thin in order to allow some light through). The family had no furniture. They squatted on the floor to eat their meals and unrolled their bedding on the floor at night. They cooked over an open fireplace known as a mud stove because it was made of clay mixed with hay. The chimney rose high over the roof to keep sparks from setting fire to the bark shingles. They had no light at night, except for the fireplace. Victoria also recalled that her family made brooms by fastening willow twigs together and gathered moss to use as diapers for babies and for wiping floors after scrubbing. Although Victoria didn't specifically mention cooking pots, her mother likely made pots of rawhide stretched over willow frames. These pots were filled with food and water, then heated stones were added to boil the water and cook the food, since the pots could not be placed directly over a fire. The first time Victoria ever saw money was when the local Cree began to receive treaty money. She wondered why anyone would need it.

Wealthier families had larger, more comfortable homes and more manufactured furnishings. François-Xavier "Little Batoche" Letendre, the most prosperous merchant and trader in the North-West Territories, lived in the grandest house west of Winnipeg. It had six bedrooms and was decorated with the most expensive furniture he could purchase in the East. The living room had many chairs, "a divan covered with rich red satin brocade fashioned with fringes of pom-poms" and one of the first pianos in the West. The floor was covered with a silk plush carpet, and a huge chandelier lit with candles hung from the ceiling. On the walls were original French oil paintings and tapestries.

Most people lived in houses considerably less grand than that of the Letendre family, but larger and better furnished than the small log house Victoria remembered. Most houses had two storeys. The main floor consisted of a large living room with a kitchen at one end, forming an L, and the master bedroom in another corner. Two or three other bedrooms were on the second floor. The wooden floors were decorated with homemade braided mats. Although the Métis largely lived off the land, there is no doubt that their homes included colourful touches that reflected their flamboyant culture.

3

The Buffalo Hunt and the Laws of the Prairie

"Once we had to camp for more than three days at the crossing of the Milk River to let the buffalo go by ... [They] kept going north like a big black river, turning aside for nothing. On the second day neither the beginning nor end of the herd was in sight."

—ISABELLE FAYANT MCGILLIS

THE NORTH AMERICAN BISON, MORE commonly called the buffalo—*buffles sauvages* in French or *boefloo* in Michif—was the Métis' major food source, and buffalo hides were an important material for making such crucial items as clothing, shelter and saddles. The Métis made use of virtually all parts of the animals.

Among the Métis, wealth was computed by the number and quality of their horses, so the owner of a fast and well-trained buffalo-runner horse enjoyed high status. The best horses responded to leg signals, because riders needed their hands free for handling their guns. The horses learned to avoid badger and gopher holes and to gallop in a buffalo stampede without being gored. They also had to get close enough to the buffalo their rider chose to shoot so that he could fire at it, but then immediately move away to avoid the falling buffalo.

The 1840 Buffalo Hunt

Buffalo hunts had become so large by the 1820s that they had to be organized like military operations. There were 540 Red River carts on the 1820 hunt. By 1840, the hunt included 1,210 carts, 620 men, 650 women, 360 children, 586 oxen, 655 cart horses and 403 buffalo-runner horses. It began in early June and ended on August 17 with over a million pounds of meat and hides ready to be transported home.

Alexander Ross, who spent 30 years at the Red River and was father of a large Métis family, described the 1840 hunt. On June 15, the first hunters and their families set off by Red River cart to rendezvous with other hunters at Pembina, North Dakota. It took approximately a week for everyone to arrive. During that time, people were in a holiday mood—visiting, gambling, drinking, running horse races, singing and telling stories. The noise was unbelievable. Horses neighed, oxen lowed, dogs barked, cartwheels squealed and people shouted. Ross disapproved, considering their behaviour "wild and lawless."

Things quickly changed once everyone had arrived. The priest, who traditionally accompanied the hunting party, presided over the meeting held to choose hunt officials and to ratify the traditional hunt rules. To Ross' evident surprise, this was all done "without the aid of writing materials."

Jean-Baptiste Wilkie was named captain of the 1840 hunt. Ross described Wilkie, whose daughter Madeleine later married Gabriel Dumont, as "a man of good sound sense and long experience . . . a fine bold-looking and discreet fellow." Ten subcaptains, each with 10 hunters under his command, served under Wilkie.

The laws of the hunt, which varied little from year to year, were strictly enforced. Three of the most important rules were: no one was to leave camp without permission; no one was to run buffalo before the general order was given; and each subcaptain, along with his men, was to take his turn patrolling the camp and guarding it at night. Penalties for breaking the laws could be harsh. For a first offence on the 1840 hunt, the culprit's saddle and bridle were to be cut up. For a second offence, their coat was cut up. The penalty for a third offence was flogging. Anyone convicted of the theft of even the smallest item was to be brought to the middle of camp and denounced three times as a thief.

A buffalo hunt, drawn by Quebec artist Henri Julien while he accompanied the NWMP across the Canadian West as an illustrative reporter in 1874 and 1875.

At dawn each day, scouts fanned out in pairs to look for buffalo and to check for enemies. Although the hunt had officially begun nearly two weeks earlier, scouts did not sight the first buffalo herd until July 4. That morning, about 400 men mounted their horses and anxiously waited while Captain Wilkie surveyed the buffalo through his spyglass. At 8 a.m. he issued the order to start. The hunters started out at a slow trot, gradually picking up speed to a full gallop. Riding in the lead were the approximately 50 men who owned the best horses and were the most experienced hunters. The herd, which was perhaps three kilometres away, did not react until the hunters had approached within 400 or 500 metres. Then the bulls pawed the ground, bellowed or twitched their tails before taking flight. Soon horses and riders were in the thick of the herd and the first shots rang out. The ground shook as if there were an earthquake, and dust darkened the sky.

The hunt itself lasted about two hours, and it took several more hours before the hunters reassembled and butchered their kills. An experienced hunter on a good horse could kill from 10 to 12 animals, while hunters with inferior horses would only get 2 or 3. The chances of injury were very high, but being attacked by an angry buffalo was not the only danger. During that day's hunt, the rocky ground and badger holes resulted in 23 horses falling, although not all of these horses, or their riders, were seriously injured. One horse was gored by a bull and died on the spot; two other horses were disabled in falls. One rider broke a shoulder blade, another lost three fingers when his gun burst and a third was struck on the knee by "an exhausted ball." Ross commented, "These accidents will not be thought over-numerous, considering the result; for in the evening no less than 1,375 buffalo tongues were brought into camp."

The remainder of the camp slowly followed the hunters with their Red River carts. Once the day's kill was butchered, the carters collected the meat and hides belonging to their families. Hunters usually dropped personal items like gloves to mark their kills. The rare cases of disputes over the ownership of a carcass were settled by dividing it among the claimants. It was critical to work quickly, as any animals not picked up before dark would be eaten by wolves overnight. Once the meat was safely in camp, the hunters could relax while the women prepared the meat and skins.

The Battle of Grand Coteau

Dangerous as it was in itself, the buffalo hunt also sometimes led to other conflicts. The Métis, through their Cree and Saulteaux mothers, were traditional enemies of the Lakota Sioux. The Great Sioux Nation is made up of the Lakota, Dakota and Nakota tribes; however, most outsiders referred to all three tribes as Sioux during the 19th century. The most serious clash between them was the Battle of Grand Coteau, in July 1851. Hundreds of Sioux warriors attacked a party of 67 buffalo hunters from the community of St. François Xavier, on the White Horse Plains immediately west of the Red River Settlement. The Red River and Pembina people hunted together as usual that year, but the St. François Xavier hunters, led by Jean-Baptiste Falcon, decided to hunt independently. The two groups agreed to move parallel to each other about 12 to 18 kilometres apart "so as not to injure each other's hunt." They also agreed to keep in touch and come to each other's aid in the event of an attack.

On the evening of July 12, the St. François Xavier hunters were camping on the Grand Coteau of the Missouri River. They sighted a Sioux camp nearby, so five scouts rode to the top of the highest bluff to check on the camp through their spyglass. They estimated that the camp held 2,000 to 2,500 warriors. While this is likely an exaggeration, there were undoubtedly considerably more Sioux than Métis. The Sioux caught sight of the scouts and sent 20 men out to meet them. Two of the scouts managed to escape, but three were captured. The Sioux pursued the fleeing scouts back to their camp and promised that they would return the prisoners the next day in exchange for presents.

The Métis did not believe the Sioux promise and began immediate preparations for an attack, which they expected would take place the next morning. They parked their carts in the usual circle, forming a corral for their horses and oxen. Then, they dug trenches under the carts to shelter the women and children, and rifle pits outside the ring of carts. The rifle pits were far enough away from the carts to keep the Sioux out of firing range of the livestock.

After dark, two men rode to ask the Red River and Pembina hunters for help. The priest, Father LaFlèche, celebrated Mass early the next morning, a Sunday. When the scouts signalled that the Sioux were coming, 30 men rode out to meet them. The Métis offered the Sioux some presents if they would release the prisoners and leave, but the Sioux refused. Instead, they charged at the barricade of carts and began shooting. The Métis shot back. Two of the Métis prisoners managed to escape during the battle, but the third was killed.

As the battle raged about him, Father LaFlèche prayed and encouraged his flock. Afterwards he told a friend that he did not have a gun, but he did have a hatchet that he planned to use if the Sioux breached the barricade. Not all of the women stayed safely in the trenches; some young women or girls waited by the men with powder horns and bags of balls to reload the guns. Falcon's sister Isabelle took one of his guns and fired it "not without effect."

The first battle lasted about six hours before the Sioux, who had suffered heavy losses, withdrew. The Métis decided to try to rejoin the main hunting party. They quickly broke camp and set off. After an hour's march, however, the scouts signalled that the Sioux were pursuing them. Quickly, they wheeled their carts into defensive mode and faced the Sioux in a second battle that lasted for five hours.

Finally, the Sioux chief rode up to the Métis and said that they were going to retreat. The Sioux had 80 men and 65 horses killed, compared to the loss of a single Métis and 16 of their livestock. The Sioux likely felt that the eclipse of the moon that occurred over the night of July 12–13 and the presence of Father LaFlèche in the Métis camp were both bad omens for them.

Isabelle Fayant McGillis was present at the battle as a girl of 13. Isabelle said that the battle ended when the Sioux chief galloped up to the Métis barricade and raised his hand in a sign of peace. The chief said that the Sioux had not known that the Métis had a "Black Robe" (missionary) with them.

"Remain in peace; we shall attack you no more," he promised as he followed his warriors away from the field of battle.

The main body of hunters and some Saulteaux allies arrived on the second day, but it is unclear whether they participated in the battle or only arrived afterwards. Another story—which seems unlikely to be true since none of the eyewitnesses mentioned it—says that the battle ended when Isabelle Falcon and Madeleine Wilkie led a group of young women who volunteered to strip and act as decoys. Each time a Sioux warrior rode forward to seize one of the naked women walking toward them, a Métis sharpshooter would fire at him. Finally, the Sioux withdrew and the women gathered their clothes about them and returned to the circle of carts. That the Sioux lost, not how the battle was won, is the important point. From that time on, the Sioux acknowledged the Métis as masters of the plains.

"An Incomparable Time of Freedom and Plenty"

Louis Goulet, who was born in 1859, looked back with nostalgia on the buffalo hunts of his childhood as an "incomparable time of freedom and plenty." He travelled with his extended family and friends "at the speed of an ox towards the setting sun through the vast, fragrant air of the endless plain that provided everything they needed to live—wild berries, fresh meat, and clear, cool spring water." Louis' father was a trader, so the Goulet family spent their summers following the buffalo hunt. They would leave their farm south of Winnipeg as soon as the grass was "nippable" (long enough for grazing) with anywhere from 10 to 30 carts of trade goods. They would return home for a few weeks in July before returning to the prairie until late fall. Some years they even overwintered on the plains. By 1868, the last buffalo herds had disappeared from the Red River Valley, and hunters had to follow the buffalo farther and farther south and west. Louis was too young to understand that an important part of the Métis way of life was ending.

Although Goulet was not born until eight years after the Battle of Grand Coteau, he recalls that the Métis continued to worry about the possibility of Sioux attacks. Goulet says that hunting parties were always "armed to the teeth [because] . . . we'd learned from experience that to be sure of peace we had to prepare for war."

The hunt laws in Louis' childhood were similar to those a quarter of a century earlier, as described by Alexander Ross. Lawbreakers were fined a certain number of buffalo skins, which were distributed to the needy or to the guards. For murder, the penalty might even be death. The most serious incident that Louis knew of involved a family named Deschamps, who were "caught red-handed breaking all the rules including the ones about robbery and immorality." One member of the family also attacked some of the councillors. The next morning, the entire Deschamps family were found dead in their tent. The Deschamps massacre became a legend on the plains, but no one ever openly admitted to having done the deed.

When the hunters made camp for the night, the carts were drawn into a circle with shafts facing outward. Then the carts were tipped up so that their shafts pointed skyward and the cart bottoms formed a barricade. To prevent an enemy from breaking through the barricade, the wheels of neighbouring carts were fastened together with thongs or by running poles through the spokes. Thus, the camp could be quickly transformed into a fortress if it came under attack.

The hunt leader, his assistant and 10 or 12 councillors were chosen in "a kind of semi-religious ceremony" presided over by the missionary priest. The council appointed sentries and scouts. The sentries were posted around the camp in two-hour shifts from sundown to dawn. At dawn, scouts went out to look for buffalo and check for enemies. If the scouts reported a herd of buffalo and the hunt leader decided that the caravan was to march that day, the leader would pick up a white flag and follow the guide. White was chosen because it was the colour most easily seen.

Antoine Vermette, one of the greatest buffalo hunters of the plains during the 1860s, also provided a vivid first-hand account of buffalo hunting. He said that their horses were so anxious to go when they saw the herd that they strained at the bit and the hunters could hardly hold them back. By the time that the chief of the party signalled them to start, blood would be dripping from the horses' mouths. Then the horses "would lay their ears back and run with their necks outstretched and mouth open, keeping up the terrific pace for mile after mile." The men did not load their guns until they caught up with the herd.

> [We] would drop some powder down the barrel of our old muzzle loaders and place a cap ready. We did not use any wadding, and supported the gun in an upright position from the saddle, so that the powder could not run out. We always carried the lead bullets in our mouths, and as soon as we were ready to fire we dropped the wet slug down the barrel where it stuck a little. Then we raced at breakneck speed until we were within a few feet of the buffalo. As there was nothing to protect the bullet from falling out of the barrel we had to throw our guns forward and shoot almost with one motion. It has happened that a man was a little slow in shooting and allowed the bullet to slide half way down the barrel before he pulled the trigger. Then it occurred that the gun burst at the centre . . . [The hunters] could drop a big cow or bull . . . with the first shot. You must remember too that this was on the run, and that we did not take any aim.

The Winter Hunt

Winter hunts were smaller than the spring and fall hunts. The artist Paul Kane observed the winter hunt at Fort Edmonton around 1848 and described how the meat was frozen for summer use. The men dug a square pit large enough to hold 700 to 800 carcasses. They paved the bottom and sides of the pit with blocks of ice cut from the river and cemented the blocks together by pouring water over them. They quartered the buffalo carcasses and piled them into the pit after the blocks were solidly frozen together. Finally, they covered the pit with straw and built a shed over it to keep off the sun and the rain. Kane thought the frozen meat was more tender and better flavoured than fresh meat.

Vermette described a tragedy that took place during a winter hunt in the mid-1860s. A hunter got lost in a blizzard, and when his body was finally found three or four years later, it was tightly wrapped in a buffalo skin. It was supposed that the hunter had wrapped himself in the skin of a newly killed buffalo to keep warm and that the skin froze solidly around him while he slept, "sealing him in a living tomb, with the white snow as a shroud."

Trader Norbert Welsh told a story about a winter hunt with a difference. During a March blizzard, a large herd of buffalo broke through the ice while crossing the river near his home. When it began to thaw, Native people cut the buffalo out of the ice and saved the hides and carcasses of over 1,000 animals.

The End of the Buffalo Hunt

Although there were at least 50 or 60 million buffalo in North America in 1800, fewer than 700 remained in the wild a century later. The last large hunt took place in 1876, when the buffalo were on the verge of extinction. The Canadian government and the incoming settlers subscribed to the British imperialist view of the land, believing that people of European (especially British) background were culturally more advanced than the First Nations and Métis, and that the buffalo should give way to agriculture. Peter Erasmus acted as a guide for Captain John Palliser's expedition through the North-West in 1857–60, which employed many Métis as guides, hunters and interpreters. Erasmus stated that Palliser believed that "a policy of buffalo extermination had been adopted as the quickest way to break down Indian resistance to American authority." Not surprisingly, no such statement occurred in any official expedition documents.

While the American and Canadian governments may have encouraged the extermination of the buffalo, it was not caused by a single factor. The increasing use of firearms meant that everyone could kill more buffalo, while westward advancement of settlement shrank buffalo habitat. Huge numbers of them were killed to feed American railway construction workers in the 1860s, and the railroads also brought in professional hunters and people who hunted for sport. Some of these men shot huge numbers of animals for their tongues and hides, wasting the rest of the carcass. Domestic cattle may also have spread diseases to the buffalo.

Native peoples did not usually kill more buffalo than they needed, and they used virtually every part of the animals that they did kill. Naturally, there were exceptions, such as one winter hunt described by Norbert Welsh in which hundreds of buffalo were killed only for their hides. His wife, Cecilia, told him that she would not dress any hide he brought in without its carcass. One day, when he brought home a hide and a choice cut of meat, he learned that she was serious. She merely smiled and kicked the hide away, so he gave it to his mother-in-law.

Patrice Fleury, who went on his first buffalo hunt in 1859, said that there was a very strict rule that all the meat and skins should be preserved before any more animals were killed. Thus, "in our party we did not average more than five or six [buffalo] a week." The hides of older animals were made into shaganappi (also called babiche). The skins were scraped of hair and cut into strips about a quarter-inch wide and then dried. Before it was used, the shaganappi was soaked in water. It was so strong that cartwheels bound with shaganappi would last all summer. Sinews were dried and "stripped into strips as fine as thread and three times as lasting" to be used to sew leather goods such as tents, clothing and pemmican bags. Even the buffalo horns were polished and mounted on wood to make coat hooks and other ornaments.

It was inevitable that a people so dependent on the buffalo for most of their material needs would be profoundly affected when the animals disappeared from the western plains.

4

On the Move:
Travel and Trade

"To be a good driver of dogs, and to be able to run fifty miles in a day with ease, is to be a great man."

—WILLIAM FRANCIS BUTLER

BIRCH BARK CANOES, YORK BOATS, Red River carts, carrioles and sledges, horses, oxen and dogs. All of these transported goods and people across the western plains before completion of the railroad in the 1880s and allowed the Métis to truly be a people on the move.

Journey to St. Paul

Norbert Welsh was only 14 when he accompanied the prominent Red River merchant Andrew Bannatyne to St. Paul,

Minnesota, as a personal assistant in 1859. Bannatyne regularly sent a train of 200 or 300 Red River carts loaded with furs to St. Paul. Bannatyne completed the necessary paperwork at Pembina to allow his carts to cross the American border, and he told Norbert that they would follow the carts the following day. The next morning, Bannatyne was seriously ill, but he insisted that they must go on because he had to reach St. Paul before his carts did. Late that afternoon, they had to cross a river. Because it had been raining hard all day, Norbert went down the riverbank to see if they could safely cross over. He found that the river was rising and the rough bridge the cart brigade had built the previous day was beginning to float. He ran to tell Bannatyne that they had to hurry if they wanted to cross over before the bridge was carried away, but by this time Bannatyne was so ill that he could not walk. He told Norbert to make camp. With great difficulty, the skinny, teenaged Norbert managed to move the 200-pound Bannatyne out of the rain from the cart into the tent. Bannatyne then directed Norbert to make tea and mix up a concoction of brandy and eggs for him. By this time it was dark. Norbert hobbled the horses and sat by the fire to eat his supper. He was getting very worried. "What if Mr. Bannatyne dies and people accuse me of killing him?" he thought.

The next morning, Bannatyne was worse. His legs were black and swollen, and he couldn't move at all. Norbert suggested that they should return to Pembina, but Bannatyne refused. He said that Norbert was brave and had lots of good ideas, so he trusted him to find a way across the river.

Norbert made a bed on the cart by weaving a long piece of shaganappi between the side rails to make a spring and covering it with straw. But how could he get Bannatyne into the cart? Bannatyne could not move, and he was too heavy to lift. After much thought, Norbert decided to try to bounce Bannatyne into the cart by quickly lifting and lowering the cart shafts. He backed the cart up to Bannatyne and shifted him enough so that his body was resting on the cart shafts. Difficult as that was, it was much harder to move the shafts up and down quickly enough to raise Bannatyne into the cart. After a few tries, Norbert finally managed to get Bannatyne's upper body into the cart. Then he pushed and pulled Bannatyne into position on the mattress and fastened him to the side railings so that he wouldn't fall out if the cart upset.

Then Norbert hitched a horse to the cart and saddled a second horse. He tied one end of a length of shaganappi to the tail of the second horse and the other end to one side of the cart shaft to keep the current from upsetting the cart. Then he jumped into the saddle and crossed the river. As he put it, "Swish! We went right across and up the bank on the other side." Norbert built a fire to dry their clothes and cook breakfast before they continued their trip. They reached Fort Abercrombie, 125 kilometres from Pembina, just in time to catch the stage to St. Paul. By the time they reached St. Paul, Bannatyne had recovered from his illness.

The Red River Cart

Trains of Red River carts, mostly operated by Métis, were the equivalent of today's long-distance transport trucks. Adapted from the carts used by habitant farmers of Quebec, these rickety-looking vehicles could stand up to the rigorous conditions of travel on rough or non-existent trails. Large, dished wheels, formed by inclining the spokes of the wheels outward from the cart body, made the carts relatively stable and easy to free if they got stuck in the mud. Built of whatever hardwood was locally available and held together with wooden dowels and shaganappi, the carts could easily be repaired without special material or tools. According to all reports, absolutely no metal was used in earlier carts, although a small amount may have been used in later years. Wheel rims were constructed in several sections with spaces between them. These spaces took up the shock if the wheel struck a rock or stump and meant that the whole rim would not have to be replaced if one section broke. The carts could be transformed into tents or boats by covering them with buffalo hides. To make a raft, the wheels were removed and lashed together concave side up. Then the cart body was set on top of the wheels and ferried across.

Carts were commonly pulled by a single horse or ox, but sometimes two animals pulled in tandem. Oxen travelled just over one kilometre per hour. Horses were much faster, but they were also much more expensive. Carts were organized in brigades of 10 or in trains that could be over a kilometre in length. The longest train recorded was made up of 500 carts. A guide walked beside the ox pulling the lead cart, and each subsequent ox was tied to the rear of the cart in front of it. As in the case of the buffalo hunt, travelling by cart train was a family affair. Many families owned more than one cart, and women commonly drove their own carts.

Travel by cart was rather uncomfortable. They had no springs, and trails were rough. Also, cartwheels made a "hellish" squeal because the axles could not be greased. Dust would mix with the grease and act like sandpaper to wear down the axle, or the grease would congeal and prevent the wheel from turning.

Dog Teams

The most important means of winter travel was by dog sled. There were two types of sled, the sledge and the carriole, each pulled by one to four dogs harnessed in tandem. The sledge, which looked much like a modern toboggan, was used to carry freight. The carriole carried one or two passengers. It consisted of a thin, flat board, bent up in front and with a straight back to lean against. Covering the front and sides was green (untanned) buffalo hide with the hair scraped completely off so that it resembled thick parchment. Painter Paul Kane said that passengers got into the carriole as if slipping "into a tin bath."

Norbert Welsh paid about $30 each for the four unbroken dogs that made up his first team. The whole outfit—sledge, dogs, harness and bells—cost him about $170. "Appearance in those days was everything," Welsh said. "If a man hadn't a good outfit, he was nothing." Welsh's dog harness was decorated with "feathers"—small sticks covered with multicoloured yarn that had wooden knobs at the ends with coloured ribbons attached. The handle of his braided caribou-skin whip was decorated with vermilion (a bright red pigment) and colourful ribbons. Each of his dogs had a brightly patterned saddlecloth and a string of bells strapped around its belly.

William Francis Butler, an Irish military officer who made two trips across the North-West Territories in the early 1870s, travelled on the Saskatchewan River for almost 50 days with some 20 different trains of dogs answering to such names as Whisky, Chocolat, Tigre and Capitaine. Butler said that an expert in dog training must be able to swear fluently in at least three different languages. "Curses seem useful adjuncts in any language, but curses delivered in French will get a train of dogs through or over any thing." Although Butler found the Métis "admirable" guides and "unequalled" voyageurs, trappers and hunters, he deplored what he considered their cruel treatment of dogs.

Paul Kane agreed with Butler, saying that he had been awakened early one morning by yelling and screaming that made him think "we were all being murdered." The women who were harnessing the dogs "were like so many furies with big sticks, thrashing away at the poor animals, which rolled and yelled in agony and terror until each team was yoked up and started off."

Kane also described a week-long trip from Fort Edmonton to Fort Pitt in January 1848 with a party that included John Rowand Jr., known as Jack, and his bride Margaret Harriott. The dogs were gaudily decorated with "saddle-cloths of various colours, fringed and embroidered in the most fantastic manner, with innumerable small bells and feathers, producing altogether a pleasing and enlivening effect." The bride's carriole was decorated with special care and was drawn by a team of dogs recently imported from Lower Canada.

During the wedding journey, a serious incident took place. A herd of buffalo came down onto the river. When the dogs pulling the lead sledge caught sight of the buffalo, they dashed after them madly "notwithstanding all the efforts of the men to stop them." Soon the excitement was communicated to all the other dogs and the whole train joined in the chase. The buffalo finally attempted to scramble up the steep riverbank with the dogs right behind them. The lead buffalo had almost reached the top when he slipped and rolled down on the one behind him, creating a chain reaction. One man was seriously injured and some of the sledges were smashed, but finally the journey continued.

A New Year's Day Dog Race

Dog races were the highlight of the annual sports day held at Fort Edmonton on New Year's Day. The factors from each

Dog sledders and team at Edmonton, *circa* 1890.

post contributed toward the prize for the driver of the winning dog team—clothing to the value of approximately $25.
Someone lent Peter Erasmus a dog team so he could enter
the race his first year at Fort Edmonton. He was convinced
he had a good chance of winning, despite his lack of experience. As he said, "Every driver has been idle, eating and
drinking to the limit of his capacity all week. Their dogs are
the same, and will be in no fit condition for a short fast race
like this will be . . . Besides, I don't drink and that's my big-
gest lead over all the others."

A pair of stakes frozen into the ice marked the starting
line. About a kilometre downriver was a set of three more
stakes. The teams were to race to the three stakes, go around
them and return to the starting line. Judges watched to be

sure everyone rounded the stakes and that no one cut in front of another team unless he had a clear lead.

Erasmus asked his helper at the starting post to hold his dogs back until at least half of the teams had started out. The helper thought that was ridiculous, but Erasmus wanted the first teams to break trail for him. By the time he rounded the halfway-point stakes, Erasmus was in third place. Soon he ran a short distance off the trail into what appeared to be deep snow. The visiting racers didn't know that it actually was overflow ice covered with only a thin layer of snow. As a result, Erasmus reached the finish line first—barely two dog lengths ahead of the Fort Pitt team.

Shortly after the race, Erasmus bought his first dog team. All the dogs were silver grey, and their harness was decorated with tassels and bells. "Train dogs like the bells and react to the decorations with quite the same human frailties as do their masters," according to Erasmus.

The Death of Blackie

William Butler's concern over the cruel treatment of dogs also extended to compassion for the plight of his horse. It was early November on Butler's trip between the Red River Settlement and Fort Edmonton when his party arrived at the point where the Carlton Trail crossed the South Saskatchewan River. He described his first view of the river, which they had expected to be frozen over.

I beheld a magnificent river flowing between great banks of ice and snow 300 feet below the level on which we stood. Upon each side masses of ice stretched out far into the river, but in the centre . . . ran a swift, black-looking current, the sight of which for a moment filled us with dismay.

With "a great deal of trouble and labour," they converted the body of their cart into a boat by covering it with a large oilcloth lashed on with shaganappi. They carried the boat to the edge of the safe ice. Then the Métis guide, Daniel, chopped away enough of the thin ice to float the boat. He got into the boat and continued chopping a path through to the open water. Soon, however, the boat began to leak. The men hauled it up, emptied it and relaunched it. This time the boat didn't leak, but darkness came on so they had to camp for the night.

This delay was particularly frustrating as they were short of food. All that remained were a little flour, tea and grease. Daniel said not to worry. He knew how to fry up a mixture of flour and fat so they would not starve. Although Butler found supper very unappetizing, he had to admit that Daniel was right. "A more hunger-satiating mixture . . . it had never before been my lot to taste."

The next morning, they set to work again. Finally, they succeeded in getting their makeshift boat, attached to a long shaganappi tether, into open water. Butler attempted to cross the river first, but the boat quickly began to take on water. He barely made it back onto solid ice before the boat was completely filled. They found that the oilcloth cover had been cut by jagged ice. Fortunately, they had a second piece of oilcloth as a replacement. Butler reached the solid ice on the opposite side of the river this time, but could not land because the current was so swift that he could not catch hold of the solid ice with his axe. Finally, he shouted to the others to tow him back, which they did with great difficulty as the line had caught under the ice.

Daniel then tried his luck and succeeded in landing safely on the other side of the river. The men cheered, but their cheers quickly turned to groans. As they hauled the empty boat back to ferry the remaining men and gear across, the shaganappi snapped. Daniel managed to get back into the boat and rejoin the other men. They returned to their campsite—cold, wet and thoroughly dispirited—where they were forced to spend a second night.

Overnight it froze so hard that the river was a solid sheet of ice when they awoke. After testing the ice, they decided to risk leading the lightest horse across. The ice seemed to bend slightly as the horse crossed the centre section, but it did not break. Butler's horse, Blackie, who went next, was not so lucky. The ice broke, dumping Blackie into the middle of the river. Reluctantly, Butler agreed that the most humane thing to do was to shoot Blackie because there was no way to rescue him. Afterwards, Butler went back to camp where he sat down in the snow and "cried like a child."

After the loss of Blackie, the other men left Daniel in charge of the remaining horses and walked to Fort Carlton to get help.

The Travels of a Little Black Mare

The Métis sometimes travelled simply as tourists to see new places. A young couple named William and Josephine Delorme made an epic journey back in 1880. The Delormes travelled east to Winnipeg on their honeymoon "with a little black horse and a Red River cart." From Winnipeg, they went on to Chicago, New York, Minneapolis and Spokane. After three years, they finally settled down somewhere in the Rocky Mountains.

By 1884, they had about 30 horses and decided to return to Winnipeg. Near Battleford, however, they got caught up in the 1885 Resistance. "I could hear the bullets flying all around me . . . I [went] to the river bank and I looked at the water. It looked like it was raining heavy. It was the bullets from the soldiers," Josephine later told her son. The Delormes came through the battle uninjured, but lost everything they had except the little black mare that had carried them on their wedding journey.

Because of the trouble, the Delormes and another family decided to return to the Rocky Mountains rather than continue on to Winnipeg. "We just tied two poles across the pony's back. There were five kids riding on those poles." The adults walked all night, and they hid in the bush during the day. It took them three months to reach the mountains. "We would chase a bunch of cattle and kill one once in a while. We had nothing else to eat but the meat . . . Our toes were sticking out of our boots. We had no dresses from walking through the bush for three months."

They settled down, built a house and "earned" some more horses. They remained in the mountains until 1889, when they again decided to head for Winnipeg because William was sick. They started across the Rockies with 40 horses, but it was hard on the young colts' feet. Josephine made little moccasins for them, but these did not last long. Shortly after they crossed the Rockies, William died. Josephine "spent" four horses for William's funeral, and she had to have the colts destroyed because "they could not stand any more walking." Then Josephine and her three children continued travelling eastward until they reached western Manitoba, where her parents were living. She still had 11 horses, including the black mare. Josephine's travelling days finally came to an end in 1903, when she and her second husband took up a homestead near the Manitoba border. The black mare gave birth to 16 colts during her life and lived to be 27 years old.

Jacks of All Trades
Most Métis were jacks of all trades. They became itinerant traders, guides, freighters and interpreters and often combined those activities with farming, trapping, hunting and

fishing. Three such men who left behind detailed accounts of their lives are Peter Erasmus (1833–1931), Norbert Welsh (1845–1932) and Louis Goulet (1859–1936).

Peter Erasmus

Peter Erasmus was born at the Red River to a Scandinavian father and a Native mother. His mother was a sister of Henry Budd, the first Native person to be ordained in the Anglican Church. When he was 18, Erasmus went to work with his uncle. He considered becoming a clergyman, but after several years moved to the Fort Edmonton area and took a job as a translator and assistant to a Methodist missionary. He was a remarkable linguist who spoke five Native languages, and over the years also became a fine horseman, buffalo hunter, carpenter, guide and freighter.

When he was in his early 30s, Erasmus married Charlotte Jackson, daughter of an HBC factor and a Native woman. It was so unusual to marry at that late age in fur-trade society that someone commented, "Do you realize that Peter is at least ten years in arrears of his duties as a married man?" The marriage was evidently a happy one, but Erasmus had given it "considerable thought" because of his prejudice against HBC factors. He believed many of them felt no moral obligation toward their mixed-blood offspring, and yet they "held themselves in higher esteem than us ordinary mortals."

Because he was a Protestant and did not have a French-Canadian background, Erasmus did not call himself a

Métis. He did, however, express a strong kinship with them in this description of a trip he made with a Métis brigade on the North Saskatchewan River:

> Someone started a French boat song . . . a rollicking melody that expressed my own feeling of the joy and freedom of the prairies. I was thrilled to be a part of this happy good fellowship of the crews . . . Fifteen or more riders appeared on the flats . . . they were mostly girls and young women. They made a picturesque sight as they reared their horses, circled and manoeuvred [them] in a wild show of horsemanship . . . Most of the young Métis women could handle horses and use a gun with facility . . . The men all cheered, lifted their paddles high in the air in a salute.

Norbert Welsh

Norbert Welsh began his formal trading career at the age of 18, when he was hired by a trader named Joseph MacKay. They travelled with 10 Red River carts and 15 horses to Big Stone Lake, about 115 kilometres northeast of Edmonton, where they spent the winter trading. MacKay's trade goods included tea and sugar, ammunition, guns, tobacco, yard goods, axes, knives and copper kettles. Welsh admitted that they also carried "the main thing," lots and lots of alcohol.

MacKay and his wife were very hospitable, and their home was always a gathering place for the leading hunters and traders of the plains. "We paid attention to class distinctions in those days, and we buffalo hunters and traders thought quite well of ourselves," Welsh wrote. MacKay was a brave and dashing figure who always rode the best buffalo-runner horse. While on a buffalo hunt he once was challenged to kill a wounded bull that was ready to charge. MacKay galloped up to the animal and drove his knife into its ribs. The knife gashed his hand badly when the buffalo reared, but MacKay got safely away. He rode back to his challenger and said, "Withdraw my knife and bring it to me if you are as brave as you say." The challenger refused, and Mackay publicly branded him a coward.

MacKay sent Welsh by himself on a short trading trip that winter with $250 worth of trade goods. He instructed Welsh to give the residents a little tea, sugar and tobacco when he first entered a camp. MacKay said that after the Natives drank the tea and smoked, they would feel that they ought to trade with him. Welsh's first trade experience was successful. He traded the $250 of trade goods for $360 worth of furs.

A few months later, in August 1863, Welsh set off in charge of his first independent trading venture. He travelled to an area along the South Saskatchewan River near present-day Saskatoon. He did a brisk trade in buffalo robes with both Cree and Assiniboine hunters, but then there was trouble. Some of the men continued to want alcohol after they had traded away all their goods. When Welsh refused to give them any more, one man slashed at him with a butcher knife. Welsh stood still to show that he did not fear his attacker and let the attacker "slash my shirt until it hung in ribbons from my collar," leaving him with scars that he carried for the rest of his life. Finally, he picked up a stick and yelled at the men to clear out, threatening to kill them if they didn't. The approximately 30 men who were in and around his house all left immediately, but he worried that they would return and attack him again. The next day, however, the man who had attacked him returned to apologize and brought furs to pay for the destroyed shirt.

The next year, Welsh married Cecilia Boyer. They spent their honeymoon travelling from the Red River to St. Paul with a train of 300 Red River carts loaded with furs belonging to Andrew Bannatyne, who had hired Welsh to manage the cart train. The return trip took 30 days, and Welsh received wages of $200.

Louis Goulet

Louis Goulet, who reminisced about the buffalo hunts of his childhood, had many other adventures. In the spring of 1881, Goulet and two friends went to Wolf Point on the Missouri River, where they were hired by the American government as scouts. Requirements were very stringent. In addition to being expert horsemen and crack shots, they had to be able to read and write English, speak at least three First Nations dialects fluently, box a little and throw a knife. Scouts also had to be at least 6 feet tall and weigh 185 pounds. They were paid $75 per month. All their equipment and uniforms were included, except for horses and saddles. They worked as policemen, detectives and soldiers, in turn. "We always had to be spit-and-polish for inspection like soldiers," Goulet said. Horses and saddles were to be equally spruce, with horses being curried morning and night.

Goulet enjoyed the adventure and excitement of scouting, but found it difficult "to remain polite and good-natured no matter what happened." Most of all, Goulet enjoyed wearing the smart, navy blue wool scouts' uniform topped with a broad-brimmed felt hat. He had always worn the latest styles of clothing made of the best-quality fabrics. "I'm not ashamed to say most people thought I was quite a good-looking fellow," he admitted.

Goulet also did undercover work as a scout-at-large among the First Nations people. Being Métis, speaking the Sioux language and knowing how to put on "a little act" were definite advantages. "Personally, I could manage very well" on all counts, he said. He posed as a trader specializing in trinkets for the women—the ideal role for a handsome ladies' man.

Goulet was 6 feet 2 inches tall and active in many sports. He was especially good at boxing. Once, in a bar in Helena, Montana, he even boxed with John L. Sullivan, heavyweight champion of the United States. The crowd was hostile to Sullivan, so his manager stopped the fight—much to the disgust of the cowboys watching it. "I came out of the whole affair with flying colours," is how Goulet described his experience.

During Goulet's time as a scout, he only had two skirmishes with the Sioux. On one occasion, four men were killed and Goulet's horse was shot out from under him. The scouts took about 200 horses from the Sioux in that engagement. However, Goulet said that if the Sioux had not been short of ammunition, "they'd have done the same to us as they did to Custer." On another occasion, 25 Sioux and 10 scouts were killed in a skirmish, and Goulet got an arrow in his leg.

Scouts signed up for renewable six-month terms. Goulet worked for three terms, but then quit because the government wanted to lower the wages rather than give the promised regular raises. In March 1883, Goulet was hired by the North-West Mounted Police (NWMP) at Wood Mountain to visit Métis from Manitoba who were now living along the Missouri River in the United States and had not yet sold their scrip. (Scrip were certificates issued under the Manitoba Act of 1870 by which the Métis were to receive title to 160 acres of land or an equivalent dollar value.) Each day the police received a list of available scrip and its value as laid down by the Lands Office in Winnipeg. Goulet went along as interpreter and guide while a NWMP captain visited the scrip holders. It was dangerous work because the American Natives were hostile to white people. "It wasn't so bad if you could speak French, because then you could pass for a Métis and for once that was a help, even useful," Goulet said wryly.

One day they saw some mountain sheep and decided to shoot one for fresh meat. All but one of the sheep ran away. Finally, they got close enough to see that a large snake was wound around that sheep and was holding one of its front feet clamped in its jaws. They shot the snake, which was 30 centimetres in diameter and measured some 3 or 4 metres in length.

From 1886 to 1893, Goulet worked variously as a freighter, railway construction worker and a cowboy. In the spring of 1893, he began having violent headaches. One day he realized that he was blind in his right eye, and doctors told him that his vision in his left eye would be gone within a few months. At the age of 33, life as he had known it was over. He was devastated and briefly considered committing suicide.

Instead, he called on the missionary priest Father Lacombe for help. By the end of ten days of private conversations in Cree with Father Lacombe, Louis had decided that his trouble "was not so much physical as moral." He underwent a religious conversion, back to the faith of his childhood. In 1900, not wanting to be a burden to anyone, he entered a residence called the Home for Incurables in Portage la Prairie, Manitoba, where he remained until the end of his life in 1936. During that time, he gained a reputation as a wonderful storyteller.

5

Remarkable People of Early Alberta

"The fort was very lively, as all were busy preparing for the great annual voyage to the coast of Hudson's Bay . . . the repacking of their furs, the launching and loading of the boats, and all the necessary preparation, gave the inside of the fort an air of business and mercantile activity that looked more civilized than anything we had before seen in the Saskatchewan."

—CAPTAIN JOHN PALLISER,

DESCRIBING FORT EDMONTON *CIRCA* 1859

FORT EDMONTON, PERCHED HIGH ON the banks of the North Saskatchewan River, was the headquarters of HBC's Saskatchewan department and the largest settlement west of the Red River for many years after its construction in 1795. Peter Erasmus was impressed with Fort Edmonton and described it as built of spruce logs extending 11 feet in the air and sunk 4 feet into the ground so "there was no moving them in any direction." There was a single entrance, built to withstand any attempt to break in, and a walkway about seven feet above ground around the inside of the stockade. Each corner of the walkway had a bastion, and brass cannons covered the south and west approaches to the fort.

A typical fur-trade season at Fort Edmonton began with the arrival of a brigade of 10 to 15 York boats from Hudson Bay in late September or early October. These large wooden freight boats were laden with trade goods and supplies. Some goods were for use at Fort Edmonton; others were to be shipped to posts such as Rocky Mountain House and Lesser Slave Lake.

Fall also was time to harvest potatoes and turnips, kill big game and wild fowl, net whitefish and make hay. The blacksmith gathered coal from the riverbank to use in his forge. A list of goods to be gathered or manufactured at Fort Edmonton over the winter of 1840 included: 8 York boats with 28-foot keels, 3,500 pounds of grease, 1,500 bales of dried meat, 450 bags of pemmican, 100 pairs of tracking shoes, 30 leather tents and 500 buffalo tongues. The women spent the winter making snowshoes, pemmican, tents and clothing.

Over the winter, the fur loft gradually began to refill as trappers brought in pelts to trade. By the end of April or early May, pack trains arrived with furs from north and west of

Fort Edmonton. All incoming furs were inspected and loaded into boats. By mid-May the York boats and most of the men had departed for Hudson Bay. The women and a few remaining men did the gardening and repair work over the summer, while awaiting the return of the boats in the fall.

The Bird Family

Chief Factor James Bird served at Fort Edmonton from 1799 until 1816. One son, James Jr., "Jimmy Jock," served a five-year apprenticeship with the HBC. A fiercely independent man who often clashed with authority, Jimmy Jock later left the HBC and lived among the Blackfoot as a freeman hunter and trapper, guide and interpreter. (Freemen or free traders, usually Métis, worked as traders, hunters or trappers without being under contract to either the HBC or the Nor'West Company.) He was temporarily in charge of Rocky Mountain House when Paul Kane visited there in the spring of 1848. Kane invited Bird to accompany him to Edmonton, since there was a shortage of food at Rocky Mountain House. They rode all day "at a tremendous pace, stimulated by hunger," until they reached a cache of dried meat that Bird had stored along the way. He had just started to remove the heavy logs concealing the cache when he heard strange noises and called Kane to come with his gun. As the top was removed from the cache, Kane shot a fat wolverine that jumped out of it. The men concluded that the wolverine had been so thin when he discovered the cache that he was able to enter it by squeezing between the logs. After stuffing himself, however, he was too fat to escape the same way he had come in. Sadly for Kane's and Bird's empty stomachs, what little food the wolverine had not eaten had been mangled and tossed about in the dirt.

The Rowand Family

For 30 years, John Rowand was in charge of the Saskatchewan district of the HBC (the posts along or near the North Saskatchewan River), headquartered at Fort Edmonton. Known to the Native people as "Big Mountain" because he was enormously fat, Rowand was a controversial figure. Some people said he was a just and well-liked man. Others claimed that he had a violent temper that ultimately killed him. HBC governor George Simpson said that Rowand had "by his superior management realized more money . . . than any three of his colleagues."

One of the many stories told about Rowand is how he found a wife. One morning he left the fort to go hunting. A young woman named Louise Umfreville watched him ride away. When his horse returned alone later in the day, she was concerned and set off to look for him. She found him lying on the ground with a broken leg. She set his leg and got help to bring him back to the fort, possibly saving his life. Soon afterwards he married Louise. She brought a valuable herd of horses to the marriage, adding to Rowand's prestige among the local people.

John "Jack" Rowand Jr., son of Chief Factor
John Rowand and Louise Umfreville.

The Rowands had seven children. Their eldest son,
John Jr., known as Jack, became an HBC chief trader like
his father. Their second son, Alexander, trained as a doc-
tor at Edinburgh University. He accompanied his father
and Governor Simpson on a trip around the world and
later practised medicine in Quebec City. Three Rowand
daughters married prominent men. Two married HBC

chief factors and the third married the first Speaker of the Manitoba Legislature.

Rowand had a passion for horses and buffalo hunting. He kept a fine stable at Fort Edmonton and even had a racetrack constructed. He also built a very large, elaborate, three-storey house that became known as Rowand's folly. The house had numerous glass windows at a time when all the other windows at Fort Edmonton were made of buffalo-skin parchment.

In 1854, Rowand, who planned to retire to Montreal, set off from Fort Edmonton with the spring brigade. He stopped at Fort Pitt, where his son Jack was chief trader. The two men planned to travel to York Factory together, picking up boats from all the posts en route. At Fort Pitt, however, a fight broke out between two men, and Rowand rushed out of his son's house to break up the fight. Suddenly, he clutched his chest, collapsed and died, likely of a stroke. There is no record of either of the fighters being punished; but rumour has it that Jack paid someone to kill the man whom he blamed for starting the fight.

Rowand had to be buried at Fort Pitt, although he had told his friend Governor Simpson that he wished to be buried beside his father in Montreal. As a result, the following year Simpson ordered that the body be exhumed and sealed up in a barrel of either rum or brine. One version of the story claims that voyageurs tapped the barrel and replaced rum with brine.

The canoe carrying Rowand's remains was caught in a storm on Lake Winnipeg, and the barrel was lost overboard. It was recovered several weeks later by a canoe brigade heading for York Factory. The barrel, supposedly marked "Salt Pork" so that the voyageurs would not know its contents, was addressed to Montreal. Because there was no direct connection between York Factory and Montreal at that time, the barrel was shipped via England and did not arrive for burial in Montreal until 1858, some four years after Rowand's death.

John Edward Harriott

English-born John Edward Harriott was the nephew of Chief Factor John Peter Pruden, the founding father of a large Métis family. Harriott became a chief factor in 1846 and spent many years in charge of Fort Edmonton. He married his cousin, Elizabeth Pruden, and they spent several years in the mountains of British Columbia, where Elizabeth died tragically under mysterious circumstances. The Harriotts were travelling in the mountains on horseback. One night they camped near the rim of a deep canyon on the Fraser River. Elizabeth, who had a baby in arms, was last seen as she went into her tent with the baby and another woman. The next morning she had disappeared and was never seen again. It was believed that she got up in the night to relieve herself and fell over the cliff in the dark. The baby, a daughter named Margaret, grew up to marry Jack Rowand. (Their near-disastrous wedding trip is described in Chapter 3.) Harriott's second wife was Nancy Rowand, sister of Jack Rowand, so Harriott married his son-in-law's sister. In his will, Harriott left Margaret £50 "to purchase a gold watch or anything she may fancy to keep in remembrance of her affectionate father."

The $50 Bride

Marie Rose Delorme (1861–1960) was travelling from Fort Edmonton to Manitoba with her family the year she was 16. They met a Norwegian-born trader named Charley Smith, who decided—before even speaking to Marie Rose—that he wanted to marry her. A year went by before he met Marie Rose and her family again. This time, he managed to get Marie Rose alone, kissed her and said something in Norwegian that she didn't understand. Being anxious to get away, she replied, "Yes, please let me go" and ran back to her family's tent.

The next day, Smith arrived bearing gifts for the whole family and invited himself to dinner. Then he formally asked Marie Rose's mother and stepfather (Marie and Cuthbert Gervais) for her hand in marriage. He added that he had asked her the previous night and she had said yes. Marie Rose was shocked. She told her mother that she had not understood what Charley said, and she certainly had not intended to agree to marry him. Smith had given Mme. Gervais a gift of $50. She told Marie Rose that she should marry him, since she had promised. "It will be a good union. He is rich."

The Smiths gave up trading and became ranchers at Pincher Creek, Alberta, after their marriage. Marie Rose lived to be 99, outliving her husband and all but 5 of her 17 children.

The Cardinal and Desjarlais Families of Lac La Biche

Lac La Biche, one of the oldest communities in Alberta, is about 220 kilometres northeast of Edmonton. Former Nor'West Company voyageurs Joseph Cardinal and Antoine Desjarlais settled there with their families sometime before 1810. By 1880, most of the 300 residents of Lac La Biche were either direct descendants of these two men or related to them through marriage.

Jacques "Jacko" Cardinal was employed by Alexander Henry at Fort Vermilion over the winter of 1809–10. At the end of February, Cardinal and two men named Martel and Clément returned to the fort from Green Lake with three sleds loaded with ammunition and furs. They had almost reached Fort Vermilion when they were accosted by 16 robbers who threatened Clément's life. They said they would not kill Cardinal and Martel because they knew them and would only rob them of their weapons, snowshoes and tobacco. The robbers said they would not take the furs as they were too heavy to carry on their backs. It is more likely, however, that they didn't take them because they knew that they would be unable to sell stolen furs. Although the robbers had made a cursory check to see that the sleds really were carrying furs, they did not find the ammunition hidden under them.

The robbers finally agreed to let Clément go with his friends, but the three men had barely got their dogs moving when the robbers called Cardinal back. "We will return all your goods if you leave Clément behind," the robbers' spokesman said. Cardinal still had a weapon, a pistol concealed in his clothes. Now he pulled out the pistol and handed it to the robber who appeared most sympathetic. At the same time, Cardinal (described by Henry as "a most loquacious person") used all his verbal skills to convince the sympathetic robber to intercede on behalf of Clément. The robber agreed. He told them to drive on, promising that no one would harm them, and they reached the fort safely.

Mid-November 1810 was exceptionally cold at Fort Vermilion—so cold that one hunter badly froze his foot, six axes shattered because they became "nearly as brittle as glass" and many canoes split. Six broken axes were a serious loss without a blacksmith to repair them or manufacture new ones.

As soon as the weather warmed up in the third week of November, Baptiste Desjarlais went hunting to get some much-needed meat for the fort. He killed two red deer, but the men who went out to haul the deer to the fort were only able to bring back one carcass. Two huge grizzly bears were feeding on the other one, and there were fresh tracks of six other bears in the area. As a result, the men beat a hasty retreat back to the fort without the second deer.

On December 30, a group of exhausted and starving men from a northern post arrived at Henry's fort hoping to purchase provisions. They had been forced to eat an old horse and five dogs during their trip. Henry could not help because his fort had only about eight days' worth of rations on hand. Scarcity of food was obviously a serious concern that winter, as Henry discussed the results of the hunt on almost every page of his journal.

Tragedy of the Traill Family

William E. Traill, son of well-known Canadian author Catherine Parr Traill, took charge of the Lac La Biche HBC post in the summer of 1874. His country-born wife was Harriet McKay, whose family had been working for the HBC since the time of her Scottish great-grandfathers.

Tragedy immediately struck the Traill family on their arrival at Lac La Biche. All three of their children had been seriously ill with whooping cough, and their baby girl was "carried off" by a fit of coughing the day after they arrived. A second tragedy hit the Traill family four years later when Harriet and all the children, including a new baby, fell ill with scarlet fever. Two of the children died. Every family at Lac La Biche faced serious illness that winter, and there were many deaths. Families were also short of food because few people were well enough to go hunting or fishing.

The Callihoo Family of Lac Ste. Anne

Victoria Belcourt was born in 1860 or 1861 at Lac Ste. Anne, northwest of Edmonton. Her father was a French Canadian and her mother a Cree medicine woman who always took care of the sick and injured on buffalo hunts. Victoria went on her first buffalo hunt with about 100 other families when she was 13. The young girls, including Victoria, had the job of looking after the fires for drying the meat. She said that the smoke from the fire added flavour to the meat and kept the flies off it.

Louis Callihoo, a Quebec-born Iroquois, went to northern Alberta about 1800 to work as a fur trader, trapper and hunter. One of his descendants, also named Louis Callihoo, courted and married Victoria when she was 17. They farmed and freighted for the HBC between Edmonton and Athabasca Landing. Victoria became an expert teamster.

After Louis died in 1926, Victoria lived alone until she was 101. It must have been a record when she and 7 of her 12 children were all receiving the old-age pension at the same time. She was very hospitable and particularly enjoyed holding open house on New Year's Day. Her eldest son would arrive any time after 4 a.m., and the remainder of her children and grandchildren would arrive for breakfast. Everyone else within driving distance would drop in later in the day.

Victoria didn't like many modern inventions, but she enjoyed listening to the radio and also had the first player piano in the area. She was 100 when she first talked on the telephone. One story is told about how she went to buy a horse from her grandson Pat when she was 90. Pat told her that the horse was 7 years old. After examining its teeth, however, she informed him that the horse was actually 12. She bought it anyway, hitched it to her buggy and drove away.

Victoria celebrated her 100th birthday by dancing the Red River jig. Back in 1935, when she was in her mid-70s, she had won a buffalo robe in a dance competition. At her death at the age of 105 she had at least 240 living descendants.

6

From Petite Ville to the Tragedy of 1885

"We left Manitoba because we were not free, and we came to this new wild country to be free. Now we have to pay to cut firewood . . . The government has made its first move against us and if we let them get away with it, there will be more laws coming."

—GABRIEL DUMONT

SMALL NUMBERS OF *HIVERANTS* HAD been spending winters along the South Saskatchewan River since the 1850s, rather than returning to the Red River after the summer buffalo hunt. In the fall of 1870, a group of 40 or 50 families established a more permanent camp there, which became known as Petite Ville. According to the 1871 census, 322 people lived in the Petite Ville area. On the last day of that year, HBC factor Lawrence Clarke chaired a meeting of all the local men. He encouraged them to give up their lives as wandering hunters and settle permanently in the area. Missionary priest Father Alexis André supported Clarke's views.

Isidore Dumont (Gabriel's father) and Louis Letendre were two of the local men who spoke in support of settling down. Dumont said that he could remember when buffalo herds covered the entire prairies from the Rocky Mountains to the Red River. Now the Métis of Petite Ville found only small herds in valleys on the South Saskatchewan River and had to cultivate the land like the white settlers in order to survive. As Letendre said, "The country is opening up to the stranger and the Métis must show his white blood and not be crushed in the struggle for existence."

The men at the meeting agreed that they should form a permanent settlement to be known as St. Laurent. The people would continue to do some hunting, but they would also farm and work as freighters for the HBC.

Clarke acknowledged their concerns over land ownership and promised to write to Alexander Morris, Lieutenant-Governor of Manitoba and the North-West Territories, requesting that he grant the Métis title to their land. What the Métis would not learn until some years later, however, was that Clarke was secretly working against land and political rights for the Métis.

St. Laurent Settlement

In 1873, the people moved to St. Laurent, about six kilometres north of Petite Ville, and Father Alexis André began construction of a church. The residents elected a municipal government consisting of eight councillors with Gabriel Dumont as president. The council passed 28 articles known as the Laws of St. Laurent, saying that they would dismantle their government as soon as Canada set up a legal system in the area. The 28 laws included the following:

Article 1: Once a month the president and councillors were to judge any cases that were submitted to them for arbitration.

Article 6: Any person who insulted a member of council "in the public exercise of his functions" would be fined.

Article 14: A married man who owned three or fewer animals should not be required to give any of them in payment of his debts, but a single man "shall be compelled to pay even to the last animal."

Article 21: Any man who "under the pretext of marriage shall dishonour a young girl and afterwards refuse to marry her" shall be fined.

Article 24: The ferry would be free on Sundays or holidays for anyone going to church, but those not going to church would have to pay "as on ordinary days."

The council also passed another 25 articles known as Laws for the Prairie and Hunting, based on the rules that had been governing the buffalo hunt for generations. Article 1 stated that each year at the end of April, a general assembly would be held to fix the date to start the buffalo hunt. Articles 2 and 3 dealt with the penalties for anyone who started on the hunt prior to the agreed-upon time.

In 1875, a group of hunters did leave for the hunt before the agreed time. When they refused to return, Dumont sent 40 armed men after them. In the name of the council, these men seized all of the hunters' provisions and belongings. Dumont later returned the seized property, but he fined one of the hunters $25. The man who was fined complained to Chief Factor Clarke. Clarke wrote to Lieutenant-Governor Morris, telling him that the Métis had "assumed themselves the right to enact laws . . . of a most tyrannical nature."

As a result of Clarke's letter, the NWMP and Canada's Governor General both got involved in the issue. The commissioner of the NMWP investigated Clarke's allegations and found them greatly exaggerated. The Governor General agreed, saying that "it would be difficult to take strong exception to the acts of a community which appears to have honestly endeavoured to maintain order by the best means in its power." Despite this support in high places, at Clarke's request Dumont received a small fine and a warning. The result was to undermine the Laws of the Prairie. Clarke, however, had gone about his work in such a way that the majority of the Métis still believed him to be their friend.

The St. Laurent Settlement expanded to include six villages stretching some 15 to 18 kilometres along both sides of the South Saskatchewan River. The land was excellent for settlement, with abundant wood for construction of buildings, for heating and for fencing. The riverbanks were high enough that it was not prone to flooding, and there was lots of hay. The people laid out their long, narrow farms along the riverbanks just as they had at the Red River and as their French-Canadian ancestors had done in Quebec. Although they cultivated some land, they mainly made their living by freighting, trading and raising cattle.

The Letendre Family of Batoche

François-Xavier "Little Batoche" Letendre founded the community of Batoche in 1872 when he opened the first store and set up a ferry in competition with Gabriel Dumont. Batoche became the principal village of the St. Laurent Settlement because it was on the Carlton Trail, the chief overland route between the Red River Settlement and Fort Edmonton before the completion of the railroad in the 1880s. Xavier soon became the most prosperous merchant and trader in the North-West Territories. He had more than 100 carts freighting for him, and once a year he travelled to Winnipeg to sell his furs.

In September 1880, Xavier ran a notice in the *Saskatchewan*

Herald announcing that he had opened his new store carrying "a full assortment of first-class . . . groceries, dry goods, provisions and general goods, all of which he will sell at the lowest rates." He also advertised "comfortable accommodation for travellers and transient guests."

The first issue of the *Saskatchewan Herald* described Batoche in glowing terms:

> A large and very flourishing settlement is being made on the north bank of the South Branch of the Saskatchewan; ten miles below St. Laurent Mission . . . The land is of the very finest quality, with an abundance of good wood and water. This settlement is bound to prosper, as most of those taking up land are practical men of ample means, who began by taking in plenty of young stock, pigs, poultry, farming implements, etc.

The Boucher Family of St. Louis

Another family that became prominent in the St. Laurent area was that of Jean-Baptiste Boucher Sr. and his wife Caroline (née Lespérance). In June of 1882, they made a 52-day trip from the Red River by ox cart, travelling with five other families. The Bouchers owned four carts and brought livestock with them. One cart was driven by Caroline, despite the fact that she was eight months pregnant and gave birth to a daughter during the trip. The following day, mother and baby were back on the road.

The six families all settled near what is now the village of St. Louis. The Bouchers, who had 15 children, built a much larger house than did most of their neighbours. They were very hospitable, so their house often served as a mini hotel for newcomers, a chapel for visiting priests and a post office. It was also a favourite location for *veillées* (parties).

Many members of the Boucher clan became active in politics or entered religious life as priests or nuns. One son became a Justice of the Peace and served in the Legislative Assembly of the North-West Territories from 1891 to 1898. A daughter, Emma, became a Grey Nun. She was very zealous in encouraging young girls to become nuns, and at least four of her nieces did so. On the other hand, her zeal caused other nieces to flee at her appearance.

The Dumont Family

Gabriel Dumont, the most famous member of the Dumont family, was the grandson of a French-Canadian voyageur who married a Sarcee woman around 1800. Gabriel was born in 1837 and grew up as a nomadic child on the plains with no formal schooling. Before the age of 10, he had his first gun. He and his brother were tending a smudge fire against mosquitoes when they heard a roar. Gabriel thought it was the Sioux coming and went to ask his father for a gun to help defend the camp. The noise actually was a buffalo herd, but his uncle was so impressed by Gabriel's display of courage that he gave him a gun. Gabriel named his new gun *Le Petit* (The Little One), a name which became famous as he gave it to every gun he owned throughout his life.

By the age of 10, Gabriel could ride and break ponies, was an excellent shot with a bow and arrow, and was a good swimmer. He soon became one of the best marksmen in the camp, and as an adult he worked briefly as a professional sharpshooter. He later said, "I fired my first shot in a battle with the Sioux when I was 12." This was apparently during the Battle of Grand Coteau.

By the time he was 25, Dumont had become such a celebrated buffalo hunter that he was named chief of the hunt along the South Saskatchewan River, a position he held for 20 years. He also became leader of the Dumont clan around that time, despite the fact that his father was still living. His large head, massive shoulders and barrel chest made him an impressive figure who seemed much taller than his 5 feet 8 inches.

Gabriel married Madeleine, daughter of Jean-Baptiste Wilkie, a leader of the White Horse Plains buffalo hunt. Madeleine had some formal education in both French and English. "She was a kind, conscientious woman who became well-known for her knowledge of medicinal plants and her nursing ability." The Dumonts were devoted to each other.

The Dumonts were wintering at Petite Ville by the 1860s and moved to the area permanently in 1868. Although diplomacy was not his strong suit, Dumont became the political leader of the community. He got title to property on the

Gabriel Dumont with his rife, *Le Petit*.

South Saskatchewan River at a place that became known as Gabriel's Crossing. Here he opened a small store, did some farming and operated a ferry taken over from the HBC. Madeleine taught school at Batoche before 1885. The family became modestly wealthy. Gabriel's most prized possession was a billiard table, while Madeleine's was a hand-operated washing machine.

The Dumonts had a run-in with a group of Cree on one

occasion. While Madeleine was alone in camp, a group of them came and demanded one of Gabriel's horses. When Madeleine refused to give up the horse, they threatened to kill it. Not surprisingly, she gave in to the threat. Dumont was furious when he learned what had happened, and he demanded to be allowed to speak at a war dance the Cree were holding that evening. "It was not brave to scare my wife. Since I married her we have always been together, and what is done to my wife is done to me," he told them.

The Cree responded that they had not done this to offend the Dumonts, but rather because it was their law that friends and allies were obliged to supply their best horses in time of war. Gabriel replied that he didn't follow their law. "If you want me to go to war with you, there will be no one in front of me when we ride against the enemy . . . as long as I am always first to go up against the enemy, then nobody should touch my horses when I am not there."

The next day, Dumont went into battle with the Cree against the Blackfoot, and he killed one Blackfoot warrior. He later said that he regretted doing so because the Blackfoot had done nothing to him personally, but he felt it was necessary to show the Cree that he was the best warrior and that they had to respect him.

In the early 1880s, the people of the St. Laurent Settlement called a meeting at Batoche to protest against having to pay for trees that they cut on unoccupied land for building or firewood. Lawrence Clarke, who was the district representative in the assembly in addition to being HBC factor, accepted the petition drawn up at the meeting and successfully protested to Winnipeg by telegraph. Five days later, he received word that the Métis of the Saskatchewan could freely cut wood for their own use.

Dumont became the military leader of the 1885 Resistance. Following the Métis defeat at the Battle of Batoche, he admitted that the Resistance was over. He and a man named Michel Dumas immediately left for Montana, where they were arrested by the United States Army. Two days later, they were released on orders from Washington. Madeleine joined her husband in the fall, but she died the following spring either from tuberculosis or in an accident.

After Madeleine's death, Dumont joined Buffalo Bill's Wild West Show, where he was billed as the "Hero of the Half-breed Rebellion." He travelled part time with Buffalo Bill for the next two years. Because he had not yet received amnesty from the Canadian government for his actions during the Resistance, he could not go to France with Buffalo Bill's show as did four other men from the Batoche area.

After Dumont's pardon in the summer of 1886, he went on a speaking tour and then worked on Honoré Mercier's election campaign in Quebec in the winter of 1887–88. The hanging of Riel was a central issue in Quebec politics at that time.

Dumont was almost assassinated in the United States in 1891. One night he was awakened by a knife blow behind his left ear. The assassin stabbed Dumont many times in the back and slashed his stomach twice before Dumont was able to pin him down. The noise finally woke people sleeping in nearby tents. They rushed over in time to see Dumont grabbing the assassin's knife with his left hand and jamming his right hand halfway down the man's throat. "When they saw me almost choking my enemy, they pulled me off him and let him go," Dumont said. "I think it was somebody after the $5,000 prize the government had put on my head."

In 1893, he returned home to Batoche and resumed a life of hunting, fishing and trapping. He lived peacefully until 1906, when he died of a heart attack.

Louis Riel, the Nolin Family and the 1885 Resistance

In 1869, the HBC, which controlled most of the North-West, sold its territory to Canada. The Red River Métis believed that they should be able to negotiate the terms under which they joined Canada with the federal government, and they chose Louis Riel as president of their provisional government. Although Riel was twice elected to the Canadian Parliament, he was not allowed to take his seat. As a result of skirmishes between the Métis and the English-speaking residents of the Red River, Riel was called a traitor and banished from Canada.

Batoche, which had a population of about 500 people by 1885, became the centre of a second Métis attempt to guarantee their rights. Commonly known as the 1885 Riel or

North-West Rebellion, many people today argue it should be more accurately called a resistance. The 1885 Resistance resulted primarily from Métis frustration with a lack of Canadian government action in giving them title to the land they had been promised when Manitoba became a province in 1870. The Resistance had a profound effect on the people who lived in the Batoche area, and many of them played a significant role in the events of 1885.

In 1882 and 1883 the people of the Batoche area had sent unsuccessful petitions to Prime Minister Sir John A. Macdonald, requesting that the government allow the Métis to occupy their land in peace and that the land be surveyed in long, narrow river lots that were 10 chains (about 200 metres) wide by 2 miles (3.2 kilometres) deep, "this mode of division being the long-established usage of the country."

Charles Nolin, who had become minister of agriculture in the Manitoba Legislature in 1875, soon resigned to sit as an independent to protest the lack of government assistance given to Métis who were trying to farm. He moved to Saskatchewan in 1879 and finally settled on a farm in the St. Laurent area. He supported the resolution to invite Riel, to whom he was related by marriage, to return from Montana to lead the Métis in their land struggle. In favour of that resolution, Nolin said, "The problem with us Métis right now is that we're like a cart with only one wheel. If we want to get moving, we'll have to find the other one we need, in Montana, beside the Missouri."

Nolin and Riel were inseparable during Riel's first months at St. Laurent. Soon, however, Nolin's support for Riel wavered because Nolin was much more politically and religiously conservative than Riel. In March 1885, Riel's council accused Nolin of treason and sentenced him to death. The two men managed to reconcile briefly, and Nolin was given two important missions. He was to deliver an ultimatum to Superintendent Leif Crozier of the NWMP and also to enrol the English mixed bloods at Prince Albert to the Métis cause.

It soon became evident that Nolin was continuing to work to subvert the Métis' provisional government, and he was arrested and jailed by the NWMP at Prince Albert. In exchange for his freedom after Riel's arrest, he agreed to be one of the Crown's chief witnesses against Riel during his trial on charges of treason. This caused much of the community to brand Nolin a turncoat.

At the trial, Nolin testified that on March 5, 1885, Riel asked him to support a plan to take up arms. Nolin refused and suggested that no one should make such an important decision for nine days. After nine days of public prayers (a novena), followed by confession and communion, each man should decide according to his conscience.

On March 6, Riel and Nolin each presented their plan at a small meeting, which agreed to adopt Nolin's plan. Riel tried to prevent people from going to the prayers. As a result, Nolin "made open war" on Riel. On March 19, the final day of prayers, Nolin and Riel were to meet to discuss the situation. Instead, Nolin was taken prisoner by four armed men and condemned to death. He was brought before the council at 10 p.m. and finally agreed to rejoin Riel's movement "to save my life." Riel then asked Nolin to deliver a document to Superintendent Crozier. Nolin agreed, but admitted that he did not keep his word. "I did not give them the document because I thought it was better not," he testified.

Charles Nolin was also largely responsible for building Our Lady of Lourdes Shrine at St. Laurent. In 1879, an Oblate Brother named Jean-Pierre-Marie Piquet arrived in the community. Piquet, who was born near Lourdes, France, personally knew Bernadette, one of the children to whom the Blessed Virgin Mary had appeared in a vision at Lourdes. Piquet began to pray at a local stream that reminded him of the stream at Lourdes. Other people gradually joined him.

In 1884, Charles Nolin read about the miracles at Lourdes and became convinced that water from Lourdes could restore the health of his wife, Rosalie (née Lépine), who had been ill for 10 years. Nolin obtained the water and Brother Piquet advised making a novena, which was done by the Nolin family and their neighbours. According to witnesses, Mme. Nolin felt a burning sensation when the Lourdes water passed over her, and the pain went away. She was apparently cured and lived for another 40-odd years before dying at the age of 79 in 1927. In thanksgiving for what the Nolins believed was a miracle, they donated a statue of Mary to be erected on the site where people had been praying. Nolin worked with the priest and Brother Piquet to build a grotto there to make the site a formal place of pilgrimage. About 500 people turned out for the first public pilgrimage in 1905. Pilgrimages have been held there annually ever since.

The Ness Family

Elsie Delorme, sister of Marie Rose, "the $50 bride," lived at Batoche during the Resistance. She was married to Justice of the Peace George Ness, who was born in South Africa, the son of a British military man. Ness was one of the nine witnesses called for the prosecution at Riel's trial. Ness testified that he first realized that the Métis might take up arms on March 17, 1885, when a neighbour told him that Gabriel Dumont was inciting the Cree of One Arrow Reserve. Ness went to Fort Carlton and informed authorities what he had heard.

The next day, Ness met Dumont with a crowd of 40 to 60 people in front of a store in Batoche. Ness made a speech to the assembled group, saying that they were being very foolish to rebel and that "they would all be killed if they went on with it." As a result of this speech, Dumont had Ness taken prisoner.

A few days later, Ness heard Riel give the order that William Boyer and Charles Nolin should be imprisoned and shot because they would not take up arms. Finally, Ness was taken to the council house for trial. The council charged him with communicating with the police and insulting Gabriel Dumont. His penalty was to have his horse, cutter and robes confiscated. Riel promised to release Ness if he remained neutral. After initially refusing, Ness decided that he had no choice but to agree. When he returned home that night, he found his wife greatly upset as she had been told that he was to be shot.

James Isbister, Founder of Prince Albert

James Isbister (1833–1915) was one of the leaders of the English-speaking Métis during the 1885 Resistance. He took up land along the North Saskatchewan River and began farming in 1862. The site of his farm, originally known as the Isbister Settlement, was later named Prince Albert in honour of Queen Victoria's husband. It became the largest English Métis settlement in the area. In addition to farming, Isbister taught school and was a lay reader in the Anglican Church. A cairn at his gravesite acknowledges him as a founding father of Prince Albert, but his role as a founder has often been overlooked in favour of the Presbyterian clergyman who founded the first Protestant mission there.

The English and French-speaking mixed-blood people were often at odds, but the lack of government action regarding land surveys united them at least temporarily. In 1884, Isbister was the only English-speaking member of the group that accompanied Gabriel Dumont to Montana to persuade Louis Riel to return to Saskatchewan. Mistrust of Riel, however, soon caused most of the white population and the English Métis to withdraw support. Isbister remained neutral during the Resistance.

Joseph McKay

"Gentleman Joe" McKay, who joined the NWMP as an interpreter in January 1885, fired the first two fatal shots at the Battle of Duck Lake, which began the 1885 Resistance. The battle resulted when NWMP superintendent Crozier met with Gabriel Dumont at Beardy's Reserve near Duck Lake. An elderly resident named Assiyiwin (Charlie Cree) was caught in the middle. McKay told him to get out of the way, but Assiyiwin indignantly refused since he was on his own land.

When Gabriel Dumont's brother Isidore intervened in the dispute, McKay drew a revolver. He fired twice, killing Isidore instantly and mortally wounding Assiyiwin. Seventeen men were killed in total during the ensuing battle, 12 on the government side and 5 on the resistance side. Gabriel received a head wound. His followers, who thought at first that he was dead, had to tie him on his horse to make certain he did not fall off as they left the battle site.

The Ouellette Family

Joseph Ouellette came to Batoche from the Red River in 1874 with four sons. The Ouellettes were among the most prosperous farmers in the area with the best herd of cattle and the most modern machinery. Although Joseph was 93 years old at the time, he played an active role at the Battle of Batoche. Gabriel Dumont and his men were holding their position on a hilltop when Ouellette was killed. Dumont later said that it was Ouellette's courage that had sustained them during the battle. "Several times I said, 'Father, we must retire.' And he answered, 'Wait a minute. I only want to kill one more Englishman.' 'Okay,' I said. 'Let us die here.' When he was shot, I thanked him and he sent me away."

Joseph Ouellette's son Moise was married to Isabelle Dumont, Gabriel's sister. Following the defeat at Batoche, Moise decided to surrender to General Middleton rather than run away. Middleton asked him to take letters to Riel and to Dumont. In reply to Middleton's letter, Riel wrote, "I will surrender, but my councillors have scattered; you must not look for them."

Dumont, on the other hand, told Ouellette to tell Middleton "that I am in the woods and that I still have ninety cartridges to use on his men."

A few days later, Moise Ouellette was arrested. He spent three years in jail and had his land confiscated, but he continued to live at Batoche and was active in the community. He chaired a committee that erected a monument in the local cemetery in 1901 to honour the Métis and First Nations people killed in the 1885 Resistance. He also was one of the founders of the Batoche Sports Day.

The Resistance and the Women of Batoche

When the fighting started, some women took shelter in the rectory; others camped on the flats east of the river or sheltered in caves dug into the riverbank. They carried food, messages and supplies to the men. Madeleine Dumont and Marguerite Riel tended the children and the wounded. Although the nights were cold, the women who were camping out were afraid to build fires. According to written reports, the Canadian soldiers treated them very roughly, even stealing money and wedding rings from some of them.

Gabriel Dumont got a leg of meat from a nearby Sioux lodge and took it to the women following the Battle of Batoche. Riel and his wife were in the group. It was the last time Dumont and Riel would see each other. Riel told his wife, "I hope God wants me to live."

Marguerite Riel had a particularly hard time. Pregnant and ill with tuberculosis, she eventually lost her baby, who was prematurely born shortly before Riel was executed. She went to live with her mother-in-law in Manitoba, where she died of tuberculosis a few months later.

Christine Pilon's Account of 1885

Christine Pilon (née Dumas) arrived at Batoche in the spring of 1882, shortly after her marriage. In an undated letter to the Bishop of Prince Albert, likely written in 1924, Mme. Pilon describes "the war where Louis Riel participated in

1885." She charged that it was not Riel "but the coward government" that "made war against the poor people of Saskatchewan." She said that the "war" ended on May 12 when Riel escaped on foot and took to the woods with his family and many others. Mme. Pilon and her 18-month-old child were in the group.

She said that Riel did not believe General Middleton's promise that nothing would be done to him if he surrendered. She quoted Riel as saying, "They will put me right in front of the cannon when I arrive."

Despite Riel's fears, the next morning the whole group walked some seven or eight kilometres back to Batoche. They went without breakfast because they had run out of food. Finally, they rested in a meadow near the village, where they butchered a calf. Riel then "bade farewell to his little children, made them pray [to] the Lord and left."

Christine continued, "We didn't see him surrender, but we heard the shouts . . . when he surrendered to them." All the houses had been burned down when they returned home. "No house, no bed, no covers. All we had left was our Canadian and Métis courage to live a season too far advanced to plant seed."

The Aftermath of the Resistance

The immediate results of the events of 1885 were devastating for Batoche. Most people had lost their homes and belongings. Families were separated and no crops could be planted that year. Almost all the adult males were imprisoned over the summer. Some, charged with treason, were jailed until 1887; others escaped to the United States. As a result, there was extreme hardship and hunger over the winter of 1885–86. Perhaps even more serious was the loss of pride felt by people who were branded as rebels and forced to depend for assistance on the government that had defeated them.

The government set up a Rebellion Losses Commission to which residents could apply for compensation for losses they had suffered or for services they had rendered during the Resistance. Most non-Native applicants received at least some compensation, but very few Métis did because the commissioners branded most of them as rebels. One exception was Batoche storekeeper Baptiste Boyer. He put in a claim to the commission for over $9,000 in damages and received about two-thirds of that amount. In his claim he reported that his store had been "completely raided of goods and furniture and all the doors and windows smashed" and that troops had taken two of his horses and two billiard tables.

Almighty Voice

One of the most notorious events that took place in the Batoche area after 1885 involved the Venne family. In 1895, a young man named Almighty Voice from the nearby One Arrow Reserve was arrested for killing a cow. He was placed in the police guardroom at Duck Lake to await his trial. A police guard jokingly told Almighty Voice that he would be hanged the next morning. Almighty Voice took the guard seriously and, not surprisingly, decided to escape. A week later, he killed a police officer who tried to recapture him. He was to remain at large for the next 19 months.

Finally, in May 1897, two young farmers named Napoleon and David Venne saw someone they thought was Almighty Voice in their cattle pasture. The Vennes reported the incident to the NWMP, and Napoleon was sworn in as a special constable. He and three police officers gave chase, and Napoleon was shot in the shoulder after ordering Almighty Voice to surrender. A party of NWMP officers and civilians arrived and surrounded the bluff where Almighty Voice was hidden. The outcome was tragic. Six more men were killed, including Almighty Voice and two NMWP officers. Venne and one other man were wounded.

7

Wood Mountain and Willow Bunch

"We were at the top of a very high hill which gave us a view of the prairie as far as the eye could see. One morning we couldn't see the plain at all, it was so completely covered with buffalo. It looked like an immense lake with a constantly rippling surface."

—LOUIS GOULET

HIVERANTS FROM THE RED RIVER had wintered and traded around Wood Mountain for many years, just as they had at Petite Ville. Many of them decided to leave the Red River permanently after Manitoba became a Canadian province in 1870. That year, trader George Fisher led 30 or 40 families from St. François Xavier on the western edge of the Red River Settlement to Wood Mountain.

By that time Wood Mountain was an important western crossroads. The last remaining buffalo herds roamed in the area. Also, the major east-west cart trails between the Red River and the Cypress Hills and the north-south trails connecting the Saskatchewan River posts to those on the Missouri River passed through the area.

Jean-Louis Légaré and the Founding of Willow Bunch

Jean-Louis Légaré was born in Quebec in 1841. He was hired as a clerk by Métis trader Antoine Ouellette in North Dakota and sent to operate a trading post in the Wood Mountain area over the winter of 1870–71. Légaré and Fisher met and decided to go into partnership. Fisher provided Légaré with merchandise, horses and carts. In return for one-third of the profit, Légaré built and operated a store at Wood Mountain. He remained the main trader in the area for the next nine years and married a Métis woman named Marie Ouellette.

When extensive prairie fires in 1879–80 destroyed the pasture needed for their horses, the people of Wood Mountain moved to form the new community of Willow Bunch. Légaré, known as the founder of Willow Bunch, continued to make trading expeditions to Winnipeg each spring with a string of as many as 100 carts loaded with furs. He was also involved in ranching, established an unsuccessful cheese factory and was postmaster of Willow Bunch from 1898 until his death in 1918 at the age of 76.

Willow Bunch was called Hart Rouge (Red Willow) by

the original Métis inhabitants and Talle-de-Saules (Willow Bunch) by French-Canadian settlers. It received its name because of the importance of willow trees to the local people. Women cut willow shoots to make baskets. Willow laths and pegs were used in house construction. The wood also was used to make pipestems, children's whistles, beading looms and frames for stretching hides. Hides and meat were smoked with willow fires. Willow bark, the original source of acetylsalicylic acid (ASA), was used as a painkiller, twisted into rope or fish nets and was one of the ingredients of the tobacco substitute called kinnikinnick.

The Cypress Hills Massacre and the Coming of the NWMP

On June 1, 1873, a group of American wolf hunters destroyed an Assiniboine camp in the Cypress Hills and killed more than 20 people. The NWMP, who had been legislated into existence by the Canadian government only a few days before this tragic event, finally arrested three men for the massacre. These men were tried in Winnipeg in June 1876. Although they were not convicted, the trial did serve notice to people on both sides of the Canadian-American border that the Canadian government was making a genuine attempt to establish law and order in the North-West Territories.

The 1874 buffalo hunt was a successful one. As they had been doing for generations, "Canadian" Métis hunted on the American side of the border that year. This time, however, American officials seized all the furs of the Canadian traders—who included François Ouellette and his son-in-law Jean-Louis Légaré—and charged them with trading on American soil. Canadian-American relations were rather complicated at that time because they had to be undertaken through British diplomats in Washington. Alexander Morris, Lieutenant-Governor of Manitoba and the North-West Territories, forwarded the details of the Ouellette-Légaré case to Ottawa. The information was then sent to London and communicated back to the British representative in Washington, who communicated in turn to the Americans. It is unclear whether Ouellette and Légaré were successful in recovering their goods.

When the NWMP arrived at Wood Mountain, they helped the local economy considerably. They provided jobs for local people as scouts, guides and translators. They also bought large amounts of dried meat, as well as hay and oats for their horses. The NWMP officers quickly came to depend on Métis knowledge of local conditions. However, federal officials did not share this feeling and showed a lack of respect for the Métis. Commissioner French of the NWMP reported to the federal government that the Métis considered Fort Pelly an unsuitable location for police head-quarters because it was in a heavily wooded area full of lakes and marshes. The government response was that the prime minister "was extremely annoyed" that French had discussed government policy with the Métis.

Sitting Bull and the Canadians

In 1876, some 5,000 Sioux (Lakota) led by Chief Sitting Bull took refuge north of the Canadian-American border after wiping out General George Custer and the Seventh Cavalry at the Battle of the Little Bighorn. Sitting Bull arrived at Wood Mountain in May 1877. There he was met by Major James Walsh, who was supported by four other NWMP officers and two Métis interpreters. Sitting Bull told Walsh that his people did not want to return to the United States because they feared that they would be killed in retaliation for Little Bighorn.

No one welcomed the Sioux to Canada. The Blackfoot were unhappy that the Sioux had moved into traditional Blackfoot hunting territory, and the Canadian government did not relish spending any money on non-Canadian Natives.

Although the American government would have been happy for the Sioux to remain in Canada, American officials felt that they had to make a token effort to induce them to return to the United States. When the American commissioners met with representatives of the Sioux and the NWMP in Canada, the Sioux treated them with disdain. They shook hands with the NWMP, but refused to do so with the Americans. After the failure of the meeting, the Americans tried to convince Canada to allow the Sioux to stay in Canada.

Newspapers in both the United States and Canada

spread rumours that the Sioux were dangerous, and people began getting nervous. The *Montreal Witness* claimed that Sitting Bull had asked the Blackfoot, the Sioux's traditional enemy, "to join him in the conflict with the hated American Government, after which he would help them with any conflict they might have with the Canadian Government." A month later, on September 25, 1877, the *Toronto Globe* warned its readers that the Métis community of Wood Mountain "could erupt at any time." The following year, an American newspaper, the *Fort Benton Record*, reported that a camp of 700 Sioux lodges was growing hourly and that four wagonloads of cartridges arrived at the camp in one day.

The NWMP investigated and found little or no substance to these and similar rumours. Walsh said it was "not natural" to suppose that the Sioux and the Blackfoot would become allies. He also maintained that police strictly enforced restrictions on the amount of ammunition the Sioux could obtain, allowing them only enough for hunting.

Just after Sitting Bull arrived in Canada, Louis Goulet was hired by American traders to build a post near the Sioux camp. One morning Goulet could see nothing but buffalo in all directions from the post, so that the plains looked like "an immense lake with a constantly rippling surface." The Sioux killed 1,000 buffalo that day, and the next day Goulet received 600 to 700 buffalo tongues in trade. This was likely the last time anyone saw a large herd of buffalo. Shortly after that, the Sioux were having trouble finding enough to eat.

Goulet became involved in a horse-stealing episode that took place in the fall of 1879. A group of Sioux stole 60 Métis horses. When the Métis complained, the Sioux promised to return all but 10 of the best horses. The Métis refused this offer. Many of the younger men—secretly encouraged by the Americans, according to Goulet—wanted to take back their horses by force. Cooler heads prevailed, and they appealed to Major Walsh for help. Walsh hired Goulet and a man named Antoine "Caillou" Morin to accompany him to Sitting Bull's camp as interpreters. They were backed up by some 30 police with two cannons and about 100 Métis who were veterans of the wars against the Sioux. "We were all on horseback and armed to the teeth. Our guns were better than the ones the Sioux had, and we weren't sorry to have this chance of measuring ourselves against Sitting Bull's braves," Goulet wrote.

On arrival, Walsh trained the cannons on the camp while the police and Métis sharpshooters spread out in a long line, looking as if they were about to attack. The Sioux came out of their lodges carrying their guns. Sitting Bull stood impassive, as if none of it was his concern. Morin gave Walsh's message to the Sioux. He told them they would have to return to the United States if they caused trouble in Canada. If they refused to go, Walsh would call on the American army for help.

The show of force was successful. Sitting Bull said, "Our only protection is in Canada where the Americans can't come after us as they'd like to. Right now, our only allies are the Métis." About two weeks later, however, Sitting Bull arrived at the NWMP barracks with his war chief, Shonga Anska, and told Walsh, "You should at least give us some tea, tobacco and sugar because we turned the horses over to you."

Walsh told him that he had to pay for whatever he wanted. Sitting Bull drew his pistol and threatened to shoot Walsh. In response, Walsh asked Morin to open the door. Then he knocked the pistol from Sitting Bull's hand, grabbed him by the hair and shoved him through the open door. Before Sitting Bull could get to his feet, Walsh kicked him in the rear.

Shonga Anska succeeded in convincing Sitting Bull to return to his camp, but the trouble was not yet over. Walsh ordered his officers to take up positions behind the stockade. Then he, along with Goulet and Morin, left the stockade. Walsh ordered Goulet to lay some poles across the road and told Morin to stand by the line of poles and tell the Sioux that if any of them crossed the line, the police would open fire on them. Meanwhile Walsh and Goulet stood on either side of the stockade gate.

Sitting Bull and Shonga Anska, followed by about 150 horsemen, advanced silently toward the stockade with its 33 men. Some 100 paces from Morin, about 100 of the Sioux dismounted and continued on foot until they reached Morin. The remaining men waited on horseback. Morin delivered Walsh's message. Shonga Anska said that the

Sioux would return to their camp if Walsh forgot the incident. Walsh agreed.

Sitting Bull trusted only two white men during his four years in Canada: Major Walsh and Jean-Louis Légaré. Times were so hard that both police and Légaré often provided supplies to help keep the Sioux from starving, since the Canadian and American governments refused to do so. By the summer of 1880, about 3,700 Sioux had returned home, hoping that they would find it easier to get food there. Sitting Bull and about 200 others agreed to return in 1881. An unknown number refused to leave, and their descendants remain in Canada to this day.

The Canadian and American governments both asked Légaré if he would help convince Sitting Bull to return home and conduct him and his people safely to Fort Buford on the Yellowstone River. Légaré agreed, and he and his men made three trips to Fort Buford between April and July 1881.

Johnny Chartrand, one of the men who accompanied the Sioux to Fort Buford, said that the first trip almost came to a violent end on its first day. Narcisse Lacert, Légaré's first lieutenant and the chief interpreter, distributed provisions that evening. The provisions included 200 pounds of flour, but Sitting Bull demanded 300 pounds. A heated argument followed. Sitting Bull finally shot at two bags of flour with his revolver. Lacert became alarmed and went to get Légaré, a "past-master at peace-making with angry Indians." Légaré agreed to hand out 300 pounds of flour.

The American government had promised $25,000 to Légaré, while the Canadian government offered a township of land for successfully conducting the Sioux to Fort Buford. Légaré sent an itemized bill for $13,412 to American officials for his expenses, but neither the Americans nor the Canadians kept their promises. The Americans gave him only $5,000 and the Canadians $2,000. It is not clear whether Légaré had to pay the wages and expenses of the eight men who accompanied him, plus provide supplies for the Sioux, out of this $7,000.

The McGillis Family

Angus and Isabelle McGillis arrived at Wood Mountain in 1870 from St. François-Xavier. The best known of their children was Angus Alexandre, who was nicknamed "Catchou," a Michif word meaning "Little Man," because he was only about 5 feet 6 inches tall. Catchou was 18 when his father died in 1881, and he became the sole support of his mother (who lived to age 96) for the rest of her life. This may be why he never married.

An 1881 newspaper story credited Catchou McGillis with killing the last free buffalo on the Canadian plains. He was known as one of the best horsemen in the area, a crack shot with a rifle and an expert with the lasso. He gained early experience working on both the Légaré and Bonneau ranches. By 1888, he had his own ranch and employees who were much older than he was. The winters of 1904–05 and

1906–07 were both extremely severe, killing large numbers of livestock and devastating many ranchers. After that, McGillis did not rebuild his cattle herd. He turned to horses and hired himself out to other ranchers. He lived to be 105, and one story says he was still riding horses at age 100.

The Willow Bunch Area during the 1885 Resistance

In the early spring of 1885, Légaré set off from Willow Bunch on his annual trading trip with 60 wagons filled with furs, hides and dried meat. The people of Moose Jaw became very nervous when they saw so many Métis camped near their town. They suspected the men were not peaceful traders, but rather were on their way to support the "rebels in the north."

Légaré told Lieutenant-Governor Edgar Dewdney that he was on a peaceful trading trip and swore his loyalty to Canada. Dewdney asked Légaré to persuade the Métis to return home, but Légaré refused. He said that it would be useless to argue with starving men and suggested the Métis be offered employment. He promised that if this was done he would guarantee that "all would be well." Dewdney sent Légaré's proposal to Ottawa, and Sir John A. Macdonald authorized the employment of 40 men to work as scouts with the NWMP. Their job would be to prevent any "northern rebel" from escaping to Montana or any people from the south going north to support the "rebels."

The meeting at which Légaré passed on the government offer to the Métis was a stormy one. The younger men were disposed to accept the offer, but many of the older ones were furious and accused Légaré of having "sold them out." They thought it was treason to take up arms when it was possible they would have to fight their kinsmen, and some opposed working for the NWMP because of their actions against the Métis along the Saskatchewan. One man actually threatened to kill the first man who took a job with the government. Another man immediately called his bluff and signed up, saying, "I'll hire on; if you want to kill me, try it." Soon 40 men had signed up, representing almost all the families in the area. They were issued horses, tents and guns. Légaré was made a ranking officer, but the scouts actually had little to do because few people passed through the area that summer.

According to another version of the story, Légaré tricked the men into returning home, and they didn't learn about the scouting jobs until after they got back to Willow Bunch. They were in a number of camps scattered around Moose Jaw, and Légaré visited each camp in turn, telling the men that he would pay them to take an important parcel back to Willow Bunch. He impressed upon them that this errand was top secret; therefore, they were to leave in the middle of the night and not tell anyone outside their camp that they were going. He told the same story at each camp, but changed one detail. Each camp was told to leave one hour later than the previous one. Légaré then hurried back to Willow Bunch, to be there to meet them. As each group arrived and realized that they had been tricked, they were furious. Some men threatened to burn down Légaré's store or even murder him. Légaré finally calmed them down and announced that the government was offering them work as scouts for wages of $2 per day. The scouts were under the supervision of the NWMP, but Légaré himself received $2.50 per day as special constable of the scouts.

The End of Louis Riel's Dream

Although the people of Willow Bunch were not as directly connected to the 1885 Resistance as the Métis further north, some sources say that they played a role at the end of Louis Riel's life. Many people were opposed to the hanging of Riel in 1885, and certain newspapers (the *Toronto Globe*, for example) speculated that the Canadian government would welcome Riel's escape from prison so that they could avoid the political consequences of hanging him. After Gabriel Dumont arrived in Montana, he worked to organize a system of escape for Riel similar to the Underground Railroad of the American Civil War. The success of the whole system rested on freeing Riel from prison, and that did not happen. Rumours persist that the jailbreak was foiled because Charles Nolin learned of it and reported it to police, but there is no concrete evidence to support this.

Pascal Bonneau, a businessman who settled at Willow Bunch after he arrived from Quebec in 1879, was supposedly involved in the abortive jailbreak. Bonneau later said that a NWMP officer brought him a message from Lieutenant-Governor Edgar Dewdney shortly before Riel was to be hanged. The message asked Bonneau to organize a plan to free Riel from prison and transport him to the American border. Bonneau hired men from Willow Bunch to post fast horses every 16 kilometres between Regina and the American border. Some people suggest that there is no evidence that such a plan involving Bonneau ever existed—except perhaps in the minds of Bonneau and his friends.

Another story says that official custody of Riel's body was given to Pascal Bonneau and that his two sons, Pascal Jr. and Treffle, helped transport it back to Riel's family in Manitoba. About a week after Riel's death, his body was finally released by officials. Immediately afterwards, at midnight on November 25, a priest read a funeral service over Riel in a local church, and he was temporarily buried under the floor of the church. Fearing that someone would try to steal Riel's body, the Bonneau brothers kept constant armed watch in the church every night until arrangements were completed to secretly ship it to Manitoba. One bitterly cold and stormy night, the Bonneau brothers wrapped the frozen corpse in a blanket and loaded it onto a sleigh to carry it to a railway siding where a single boxcar had been shunted. One or both brothers travelled with the body on its trip to Manitoba and handed it over to the Riel family.

Ranching, Racing and Rodeos

The end of the Resistance coincided with the disappearance of the buffalo from the western plains. Being skilled horsemen whose wealth was computed by the number and quality of their horses, many of them went into ranching after the end of the buffalo hunt. In 1884, Jean-Louis Légaré drove 100 horses to Winnipeg and brought back 45 head of cattle in exchange. In 1886, NWMP superintendent Jarvis reported that the Home Land and Cattle Company from Missouri had imported 6,000 cattle and 250 horses into Canada. These cattle were pastured near the Wood Mountain NWMP post. Légaré, Catchou McGillis and Pascal Bonneau Jr. were three of the largest ranchers in the area.

Local people also bred and trained racehorses, and racing was an important entertainment. Bedick was a famous racehorse who belonged to André Gaudry of Willow Bunch. In January 1885, a man named Caplette challenged Gaudry to a race. Before they could hold the race, men had to clear snow to make a one-and-a-quarter-mile track. By the time all the preparations were made, Bedick had taken sick and Gaudry wanted to stop the race, but Caplette refused. When Bedick was beaten, there was almost a war between the supporters of Caplette and those of Gaudry. The police stepped in and helped to give Bedick a second chance. The police vet treated him and fed him grain for two weeks until he was ready to race again. Bedick won the second race. Caplette complained, so a third race—which Bedick also won—was held.

The Wood Mountain Sports and Stampede is the longest continuously running rodeo in Canada. The forerunner of the stampede began on July 1, 1886, when all of the NWMP troopers stationed at Wood Mountain celebrated Canada's birthday with a sports day. It included some competitions involving horsemanship, although they were not true rodeo events. In "Indian wrestling," two bareback riders rushed at each other, each trying to pull the other from his horse. In another competition, riders had to snatch up articles from the ground while their horses were at full gallop. In 1894, the first horse races were held. They were hotly contested by both police and civilian riders. A novelty slow race was also held. Competitors entered their slowest horses (usually draft animals), but no one could ride his own horse. The riders drew the name of the horse they would ride from a hat. The winner was the rider of the fastest slow horse.

The first true rodeo event, jackpot bronco riding, began in 1905 when local ranchers brought their wildest broncos to the sports grounds and challenged cowboys to ride them. Broncos were held by the ears while being saddled and mounted. Since there was no fenced arena, a rider called the hazer kept the bronco within bounds. The cowboy who could ride a horse to a standstill won all the money in the jackpot.

When the NWMP arrived in the West, they acquired many of their horses from the Métis. The police were a bit concerned when they discovered that the leader of the guides who they had hired for their westward march weighed about 300 pounds and was more than six feet tall. How would they provide a horse suitable for a man his size? They need not have worried. He brought his own stocky horses, known as cayuses, which had no problem carrying him.

One night during the NWMP's famous March West a severe thunderstorm occurred. Torrential rain and hail fell. Strong winds uprooted trees and blew apart the police campsite. It took several days of hard riding to round up all of the missing horses. Some had travelled more than 30 kilometres south of the American border. The police soon realized that only the eastern horses had bolted. The Métis horses had stayed put.

Some people suggest that the famed RCMP Musical Ride may have been inspired, at least in part, by the Métis exercising their horses to music. The Métis also enjoyed displaying their riding ability on special occasions. One group put on an impressive display of horsemanship on the first day of Treaty Four negotiations in September 1874. They came forward "in martial array" led by an enormous man smartly dressed in traditional Métis style and mounted on a splendid dark brown buffalo-runner horse. The man wore a bright blue capote decorated with brass buttons and fastened with a colourful sash. On his feet he wore beaded deerskin moccasins. His horse had a saddle elaborately decorated with floral beadwork in the Red River or Métis style. Horse and rider curvetted about, far in advance of their fellows. The horse reared up on his hind legs, then leapt forward and raised his hind legs again before his front ones hit the ground. Next, horse and rider inscribed large circles at both a gentle gallop and a lope. Finally, the leader motioned the other riders to advance, and the whole group paraded like a cavalry troop on inspection in front of the government officials, militiamen and First Nations people in attendance.

The Willow Bunch Giant

Edouard Beaupré (1881–1904), the most famous son of Willow Bunch, was the oldest of 20 children. His father was a French Canadian, and his mother was from a Red River Métis family. Edouard's godfather was Jean-Louis Légaré. Although legend has it that Edouard weighed between 9 and 14 pounds at birth, he grew normally for the first few years of his life. By age 9, however, he was 6 feet tall. At 12, he was 6 feet 6 inches. At his death, he was 8 feet 3 inches, weighed 375 pounds, and was still growing. This made him the fourth tallest man in recorded history.

Beaupré left school at age 15 to follow his dream of becoming a cowboy. He worked on several local ranches and became a skilled rider and roper. Sadly, however, he had to give up his dream at age 17. He could no longer ride a horse because he was too heavy and his feet touched the ground when he was in the saddle. He also had his nose (and possibly other bones) broken when a horse kicked him in the face. Other sources claim that his face was scarred by a tumorous growth.

Beaupré's strength matched his size. He was known to pick up children who teased him and place them on a roof to teach them a lesson. One time, on a trip to Moose Jaw, he pulled a wagon and team of horses out of a mud hole.

In 1898, André Gaudry (the owner of the racehorse Bedick) suggested that Beaupré could earn money to help his family by going on tour to perform strongman feats. Gaudry and Albert Légaré (Jean-Louis' son) accompanied him on his first tour of the North American freak-show circuit. He visited Winnipeg and Montreal and American cities from New York to California. One of his main feats was lifting a horse onto his shoulders.

After this initial tour, Edouard and his father went to New York and other cities in the winter of 1900–01. Edouard soon had an agent and a regular job with a circus touring across North America. He didn't enjoy touring, but felt that he had to continue in order to help his family financially.

Beaupré's size required many adjustments in his daily life. The staff of a Winnipeg hotel removed the foot of the bed and used trunks to support a second mattress to accommodate his length. The cooks also provided him with "several complete meals at each sitting." A man recalled watching Beaupré lift his luggage out of the overhead rack on a train without getting up from his seat.

In 1902, Beaupré was challenged to wrestle against the

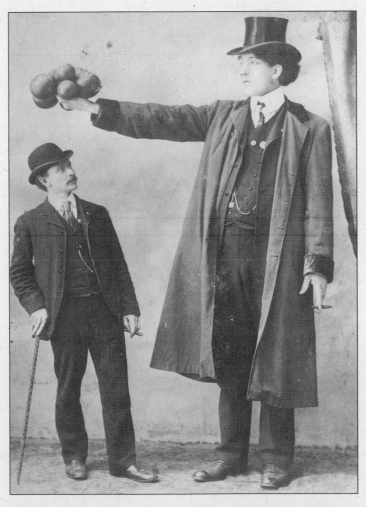

Edouard Beaupré in a promotional studio photo, apparently holding some dumbbells. Merchants provided Beaupré with free clothing because it was good advertising; thus, he was always very well dressed.

French-Canadian strongman Louis Cyr, who had the title "World's Strongest Man of All Ages." Beaupré was soundly beaten because his strength was diminishing due to the onset of tuberculosis. Doctors told him his illness was incurable, but he refused to return home to spend his remaining days with his family.

He toured with the Barnum and Bailey Circus. On July 3, 1904, at the age of 23, while doing a show at the Louisiana Purchase Exposition (St. Louis World Fair), Beaupré collapsed and died of a massive pulmonary hemorrhage. His relatives claimed that his manager exploited him by keeping him drunk and not giving him a fair share of the alleged fortune he earned.

After Beaupré's death, his agent had his body embalmed, apparently expecting that the circus would pay for the embalming and to ship the body home. The circus refused, and the agent put the body on exhibit to recoup the embalming fees. Beaupré's father started for St. Louis to get his son's remains, but returned home after reaching Winnipeg, having discovered that he did not have enough money to ship the body home. According to one of Beaupré's nephews, money likely was not the only issue. The St. Louis doctors said they wanted to keep the corpse for research, and they could do so because the family had not claimed it quickly enough.

Pascal Bonneau went to St. Louis and had Beaupré's body shipped to Montreal around 1905. It was on display at a Montreal museum for over six months before municipal authorities finally stopped the visits. In 1907, some children found the body in a warehouse. It was then sent to the University of Montreal where it was displayed in the faculty of medicine until the 1970s. Scientists determined that Beaupré suffered from pituitary gigantism, a condition that today could likely be corrected by surgery or medication.

Beaupré's family assumed he had been buried shortly after his death. In the early 1970s, his descendants were shocked to learn that that their uncle was on display in Montreal. "They had him in a glass case. He was naked," his nephew Ovila Lesperance said. The university refused to give up the body, but they did take it off display.

In 1989, the university finally agreed have the body cremated and released to the family. On July 7, 1990, exactly 86 years and 3 days after his death, Edouard Beaupré's remains were buried in front of a life-sized fibreglass statue of him at a Beaupré family reunion in Willow Bunch.

Epilogue

IN THE EARLY 21ST CENTURY, the Métis of the western plains still exist as a separate and unique people. Saskatchewan and Alberta both have active provincial Métis organizations: Métis Nation-Saskatchewan (MNS) and Métis Nation of Alberta (MNA). Membership in the MNA has grown by almost 300 percent in the last decade, and many people who remember life in western Canada a generation or two ago would agree that there has been a recent resurgence of Métis pride. Although many Métis have always taken pride in their heritage, others have ignored or denied it because of the racism they suffered from the general population. In recent years, some people have been surprised to learn as adults that they were Métis rather than French Canadian.

Epilogue

In 1991, MNS established a senate of elders. The senators guide the elected MNS leadership, providing advice and historical understanding, acting in a quasi-judicial role to resolve disputes and overseeing elections and ceremonial events. Over the past few decades, Métis organizations have been fighting for the legal right to fish or hunt for food (harvester rights). In 2003, the Supreme Court of Canada ruled in favour of such rights for the Métis community of Sault Ste. Marie, Ontario, on the basis of Section 35 of the Constitution Act of 1982, which states that existing treaty and aboriginal rights are "hereby recognized and affirmed." However, some provincial governments are still unwilling to accept this right.

The list that follows includes many accomplished Métis individuals whose stories are told in the preceding pages, as well as some of their well-known descendants. Their ranks include politicians, members of the military, a musician, a clergyman, an architect and an NHL hockey player.

And what of the Métis from my hometown of Cochin, Saskatchewan? Over the last half century some have owned small farms, ranches or riding stables. Others have worked as labourers for local market gardeners, for other farmers or in the tourist industry. Many have left rural life behind and have a variety of jobs in urban centres across the country—just like Canadians in general—taking their talents and heritage into the future.

List of Characters

Beaupré, Edouard (1881–1904): The giant strongman born at Willow Bunch.

Bird Family: James Curtis Sr. (1773–1856) was an HBC chief factor in the Saskatchewan district. One of his sons, James Jr. "Jimmy Jock" (1798–1892), was a fur trader, interpreter and guide who spent much of his life among the Blackfoot of Alberta.

Boucher Family: Jean-Baptiste Sr. and Caroline (née Lespérance) arrived in the St. Laurent Settlement from the Red River in 1882. The family has been prominent ever since. One grandson was Senator William Albert "Boss" (1889–1976), who spent 16 years in municipal politics before being elected as a Member of Parliament in 1948. He worked to gain recognition of the early settlers and of the rights of the Métis. In January 1957, he was named to the Canadian Senate. Another grandson, Monseigneur Joseph Alfred (1901–1974), was ordained as a priest in 1927 and served for more than 25 years at Sacred Heart Cathedral in Prince Albert. He often visited his childhood home and raised purebred cattle there as a hobby. In more recent times, Réal Boucher retired from the Canadian Armed Forces as a colonel in 1982. Currently, John B. Boucher is a MNS senator and was awarded the Order of Canada in 2002.

Boyer Family: Baptiste Sr. established a store in Batoche in 1883. Baptiste Jr. (commonly known as J.B.) married Virginia, daughter of Charles and Rosalie Nolin, in 1892. Baptiste Jr. and two of his sons enlisted in the First World War. In 1923, they moved to Cochin to land received from the Soldier's Settlement Board. A grandson, Albert "Hap" Boyer, a former member of the Canadian Armed Forces, won 60 old-time fiddling competitions. He was appointed a MNS senator in 2001.

Callihoo Family: Victoria (née Belcourt) (*circa* 1860–1965) married

List of Characters

Louis Callihoo, grandson of an Iroquois from Quebec. They spent their lives in the Lac Ste. Anne area of Alberta, where they farmed and worked as freighters for the HBC.

Cardinal Family: Joseph, a former Nor'West voyageur, settled in the Lac La Biche area of Alberta before 1810. The noted architect Douglas Cardinal, who was born in Calgary in 1934, is a descendant.

Delorme Family: Marie Rose Smith and Elsie Ness were daughters of Urbain Delorme, who died at a young age. Charlie Delorme, who settled on a ranch in the Cochin area in 1904, carried mail and served as a guide and scout for the NWMP and the army during the 1885 Resistance. The first school in the Cochin area was named after him. Ron Delorme, one of his great-grandsons, played hockey in the NHL between 1976 and 1985

Desjarlais Family: One of the founding families of Lac La Biche, along with the Cardinals.

Dumont, Gabriel (1837–1906): Leader of the South Saskatchewan River buffalo hunt for nearly 20 years and military leader during the 1885 Resistance. His wife was Madeleine, daughter of Jean-Baptiste Wilkie.

Erasmus, Peter (1833–1931): A hunter, interpreter, teacher and trader born at the Red River, who spent most of his life in Alberta.

Falcon, Jean-Baptiste: Captain of the buffalo hunters involved in the Battle of Grand Coteau.

Fidler, Peter (1769–1822): English-born HBC trader and surveyor and the father of large mixed-blood family.

Gaudry, André: A rancher at Willow Bunch who accompanied Edouard Beaupré on his first tour and was owner of the famed racehorse Bedick.

Goulet, Louis (1859–1936): A trader, scout and adventurer who became blind at the age of 33.

Harmon, Daniel (1778–1843) and **Lisette** (née Duval): An American-born fur trader who spent many years on the Saskatchewan before retiring to Montreal with his Métis wife, Lisette.

Harriott, John Edward (1797–1866): English-born HBC chief factor and nephew of John Peter Pruden. His first marriage was to his cousin, Elizabeth Pruden; his second marriage was to Nancy Rowand.

Isbister, James (1833–1915): The leader of the English Métis at the time of the 1885 Resistance and a founder of Prince Albert, Saskatchewan.

LaFlèche, Louis François: A missionary priest with a Métis background from Quebec who was present at the Battle of Grand Coteau.

Légaré, Jean-Louis (1841–1918): The Quebec-born founder of Willow Bunch.

Letendre Family: Jean-Baptiste *dit* Batoche (1762–1827) arrived in the North-West from Quebec in the 1780s as a voyageur. His grandson François-Xavier (*circa* 1841–1901) was the founder of Batoche.

McGillis Family: Angus and Isabelle (née Fayant) arrived at Willow Bunch from White Horse Plains in 1870. Their son Catchou became a rancher in the area. The McGillis brothers and Isabelle were all at the Battle of Grand Coteau.

MacKay, Joseph: An Alberta-based trader and early employer of Norbert Welsh.

McKay, "Gentleman Joe": NWMP interpreter who fired the first fatal shot at the Battle of Duck Lake during the 1885 Resistance.

Ness, George and **Elsie** (née Delorme): George was a Justice of the Peace at Batoche during the 1885 Resistance. The couple moved to Jackfish Lake, north of Cochin, in 1894, and some descendants still live there.

Nolin, Charles (1837–1907) and **Rosalie** (née Lépine): Charles was briefly Manitoba's minister of agriculture before moving to the St. Laurent Settlement. He testified against Louis Riel at the trial which condemned the Métis leader to death. Their daughter married Baptist Boyer Jr.

Ouellette Family: Joseph was killed at the Battle of Batoche at the age of 93. His son Moise was married to Gabriel Dumont's sister Isabelle.

Pruden, John Peter: English-born HBC chief factor and father of Elizabeth Harriott. At least two of his grandsons were freighters and another was left in charge of the HBC post at Lac la Biche during the Resistance. Some of his descendants settled in the Cochin area afterwards.

Riel, Louis (1844–1885) and **Marguerite** (née Monet *dite* Bellehumeur): Métis political leader during the 1885 Resistance.

Rowand Family: John (1787–1854) spent most of his career in charge of the HBC's Saskatchewan district, based at Fort Edmonton. He was married to Louise Umfreville. Their son John Jr., known as Jack, married Margaret, daughter of John Edward Harriott and Elizabeth Pruden.

Smith, Charley and **Marie Rose** (née Delorme): Ranchers at Pincher Creek, Alberta.

Traill, William and **Harriet** (née McKay): An HBC employee and son of author Catherine Parr Traill, William moved to Lac La Biche in 1874.

Welsh, Norbert (1845–1932): A trader in Saskatchewan.

Wilkie, Jean-Baptiste: Captain of the White Horse Plains buffalo hunters for many years. His daughter Madeleine married Gabriel Dumont.

Bibliography

Books, periodicals and other print documents

Anick, N. *The Métis of the South Saskatchewan*, vol. 1. Parks Canada Manuscript Report, no. 364, 1976.

Batoche NHS: Background Information Package and Identification of Planning Issues, n.d.

Beal, Bob, and Rod Macleod. *Prairie Fire: The 1885 North-West Rebellion.* Edmonton: Hurtig, 1984.

Bradford, Sheila. "Artifact Analysis of Boyer's Store, Batoche National Historic Site." Environment Canada, Microfiche Report Series #412, 1987.

Brown, Jennifer S.H. *Strangers in Blood: Fur Trade Families in Indian Country.* Vancouver: UBC Press, 1990.

Butler, William Francis. *The Great Lone Land: A Narrative of Travel and Adventure in the North-West of America.* 1872. Reprint, Edmonton: Hurtig, 1968.

Campbell, Marjorie Wilkins. *The Saskatchewan: The Great Rivers of Canada.* 1950. Reprint, Toronto: Clarke, Irwin, 1982.

Charette, Guillaume. *Vanishing Spaces: Memoirs of Louis Goulet, a Prairie Métis.* Translated by Ray Ellenwood. Winnipeg: Bois-Brûlé, 1976.

Dumont, Gabriel. *Gabriel Dumont Speaks.* Translated by Michael Barnholden. Vancouver: Talonbooks, 1993.

Erasmus, Peter. *Buffalo Days and Nights.* As told to Henry Thompson. 1976. Reprint, Calgary: Fifth House, 1999.

Friesen, Victor Carl. *Where the River Runs: Stories of the Saskatchewan and the People Drawn to Its Shores.* Calgary: Fifth House, 2001.

Bibliography

Gilman, Rhoda R., Carolyn Gilman, and Deborah M. Stultz. *The Red River Trails: Oxcart Routes between St. Paul and the Selkirk Settlement 1820–1870*. St. Paul: Minnesota Historical Society Press, 1979.

Hamilton, Zachary Macaulay, and Marie Albina Hamilton. *These Are the Prairies*. Regina: School Aids and Text Book Publishing, 1948.

Howard, Joseph. *Strange Empire: Louis Riel and the Métis People*. Toronto: James, Lewis and Samuel, 1974.

Indian Land Treaty No. 4. Provincial Archives of Manitoba (PAM) MG1, A 7:2.

Kane, Paul. *Wanderings of an Artist among the Indians of North America*. 1925. Reprint, Mineola, NY: Dover Publications, 1996.

Lavigne, Solange. *Kaleidoscope: Many Cultures-One Faith: The Roman Catholic Diocese of Prince Albert 1891–1991*. Prince Albert: Diocese of Prince Albert, 1990.

MacEwan, Grant. . . . *And Mighty Women Too: Stories of Notable Western Canadian Women*. Saskatoon: Western Producer Prairie Books, 1975.

MacGregor, James G. *Peter Fidler: Canada's Forgotten Explorer 1769–1822*. 1966. Reprint, Calgary: Fifth House, 1998.

Macleod, Margaret, ed. *The Letters of Letitia Hargrave*. Toronto: Champlain Society, 1947.

McLean, Don. *Fifty Historical Vignettes: Views of the Common People*. Regina: Gabriel Dumont Institute, 1987.

Rivard, Ron, and Catherine Littlejohn. *The History of the Métis of Willow Bunch*. Saskatoon: privately printed, 2003.

Robinson, Henry Martin. *The Great Fur Land or Sketches of Life in Hudson's Bay Territory*. New York: Putnams, 1879.

Ross, Alexander. *Red River Settlement, Its Rise, Progress and Present State*. London, 1856.

Sanderson, George William. "Through Memories Windows." Unpublished. Provincial Archives of Manitoba.

Shulman, Martin and Don McLean, "Lawrence Clarke: Architect of Revolt," *Canadian Journal of Native Studies*, vol. 3, no. 1 (1983): 57–68.

Siggins, Maggie. *Riel: A Life of Revolution*. Toronto: Harper-Collins, 1994.

Spry, Irene M. *The Palliser Expedition: the Dramatic Story of Western Canadian Exploration 1857–1860*. 2nd ed. Saskatoon: Fifth House, 1995.

Van Kirk, Sylvia. *Many Tender Ties: Women in Fur-Trade Society, 1670–1870*. Winnipeg: Watson & Dwyer, 1980.

Welsh, Norbert. *The Last Buffalo Hunter*. As told to Mary Weekes. New York: T. Nelson & Sons, 1939. Reprint, Saskatoon: Fifth House, 1994.

Internet documents and websites

"Agriculture" (Victoria Callihoo). http://www.albertasource.ca/metis/eng/beginnings/metis_nw_agriculture.htm.

Alberta Heritage. http://www.abheritage.ca/alberta/fur_trade/site_profiles_laclabiche.html.

Anderson, Ian. "Sitting Bull and the Mounties." Originally published in *Wild West*, Feb. 1998. http://www.thehistorynet.com/we/blsittingbullandthemounties/index1.html.

Angelhair. "The decimation of the Plains Buffalo during the late 1800s brought this magnificent animal to the brink of extinction." Geocities.http://geocities.com/SoHo/Atrium/4832/buffalo3.htm.

Angelhair. "The Involvement of the Métis Nation in the Pemmican Trade was an historic era in Canada and the United States." Geocities. http://geocities.com/SoHo/Atrium/4832/buffalo3.html.

Bolton, David. "The Red River Jig." *Manitoba Pageant* 7, no. 1 (Sept. 1961), also at http://www.mhs.mb.ca/docs.pageant.

Brehaut, Harry Baker, "The Red River Cart and Trails: The Fur Trade." Manitoba Historical Society Transactions. http://www.mhs.mb.ca/docs/transactions/.

Bibliography

"Catchou McGillis." The History of Willow Bunch. http://thewillowtree.turtle-mountain.com.

"Chronological History of the Lac La Biche Mission." History of Lac La Biche. http://collections.ic.gc.ca/laclabiche/.

Clipsham, Muriel. "A Métis Journey." Televar. http://www.televar.com/~gmorin/vermette.htm.

Dorion, Leah, and Michael Relland. "Biographies of Métis Community Leaders." Virtual Museum of Métis History and Culture. http://www.metismuseum.ca.

Dictionary of Canadian Biography Online. http://www.biographi.ca.

"Edouard Beaupré: The Willow Bunch Giant." Willow Bunch Museum. http://collections.ic.gc.ca.

"A Fur Trade Season at Fort Edmonton." Government, Edmonton, Alberta. http://www.gov.edmonton.ab.ca/fort/1846/fur_trade_season.html.

Gottfred, A.; "Femmes du Pays: Women of the Fur Trade, 1774–1821" (Art. II); "The Legend of the Pickled Factor" (Art. IV); *The Northwest Journal*, 1994-2002. http://northwestjournal.ca.

Haag, Larry. "Alexandre 'Catchou' McGillis," "Heroines of Batoche," "Isabelle (Fayant) McGillis," Métis Resource Centre. http://www.metisresourcecentre.mb.ca/.

Hall, Frank. "Manitoba's Own Mounties". *Manitoba Pageant*. Autumn 1973. http://www.mhs.mb.ca/docs/pageant.

"Jean-Louis Légaré: Founder of Willow Bunch." Willow Bunch Museum. http://collections.ic.gc.ca.

Liboiron, Henri, and Bob St. Cyr. "Experiments in Pemmican Preparation." http://collections.ic.gc.ca/notukeu/pemmican.el.htm.

"Marie Rose Delorme-Smith 1861–1960." Métis Resource Centre. http://www.metisresourcecentre.mb.ca/.

Morton, William. "The Battle at the Grand Coteau: July 13 and 14, 1851." Manitoba Historical Society Transactions. http://www.mhs.mb.ca/docs/transactions/.

Noel, Lynn. "Lisette's Journey: the Life and Travels of Lisette Duval (Laval) Harmon 1791–1862." http://www.homepage.mac.com/lynnoel/pubs/Lisettes_Journey.html.

"Our Lady of Lourdes Shrine—St. Laurent de Grandin." Western Development Museum. http://www.wdmprairiegamble.com/story/display_story.php?long_story=yes&story_id=41.

Payment, Diane. "Christine Dumas Pilon: Her Story (1862-1954)." Métis Resource Centre. http://www.metisresourcecentre.mb.ca/.

Préfontaine, Darren R. "The Sash." The Virtual Museum of Métis History and Culture. http://www.metismuseum.ca/resource.

Rock, Bob. "Moise Ouellette—the Forgotten Soul: A Tribute to My Great-Great-Grand-Father." Saskatchewan Schools. http://www.saskschools.ca.

"Testimony of Charles Nolin in the trial of Louis Riel" and "Testimony of George Ness in the trial of Louis Riel." University of Missouri-Kansas City Law School. http://www.lawumkc.edu/Faculty/projects/ftrials/riel.

"Trading with Sir John." Virtual Saskatchewan. http://www.virtualsk.com/current_issue/.

Traill, W.E. "Letters of W.E. Traill, 1874–1881." History of Lac La Biche. http://collections.ic.gc.ca/laclabiche/.

"Treffle Bonneau." Archives Chez-Alice. http://archives.chez-alice.fr/sarhissimo/xoom/catchou3.htm.

Vermette, Antoine. "Antoine Vermette, Red River Pioneer." Televar. http://www.televar.com~gmorin/vermette.htm.

Index

Acknowledgements

Thanks to the following individuals and organizations that assisted me in researching this book: Alice M. Gaudet and the Association Culturelle de Bellevue Inc. for information on Petite Ville; Rachelle Gareau and David Venne at the Batoche National Historic Site; Albert "Hap" Boyer for the interview about his family, the Boyers and Nolins; Celine Perillat at the Duck Lake Regional Interpretive Centre; Susan Robertson at Grasslands National Park for information on southern Saskatchewan; the Provincial Archives of Manitoba; and archivist Yvette Gareau at the Roman Catholic Diocese of Prince Albert for information on the Boucher, Nolin and Gareau families.

I am indebted to the authors of the many books and articles listed in the bibliography. I would like to further acknowledge the following sources: Muriel Clipsham, "A Métis Journey," for the story of the little black mare in Chapter 4; A. Gottfred, "The Legend of the Pickled Factor," for the account of John Rowand's death in Chapter 5; the Métis Resource Centre, "Marie Rose Delorme-Smith, 1861–1960," for the story of the $50 bride in Chapter 5; and Martin Shulman and Don McLean, "Lawrence Clarke: Architect of Revolt," and Solange Lavigne, *Kaleidoscope,* for the history of the establishment of the St. Laurent Settlement in Chapter 6.

About the Author

Irene Ternier Gordon, who now lives along the historic Assiniboine River just west of Winnipeg, grew up on a farm in the Cochin district north of North Battleford, Saskatchewan. She has had a passion for history, reading and writing since childhood. After a career as a teacher-librarian, she became a freelance writer in 1998. Irene has written five books, including *The Battle of Seven Oaks: And the Violent Birth of the Red River Settlement* and *Marie-Anne Lagimodière: The Incredible Story of Louis Riel's Grandmother*.

Irene and her husband, Don, enjoy travelling, canoeing, hiking, skiing and sailing. Above all, she likes to spend time with her three young grandsons: Jesse, Riley and Felix.